CHILD SAFETY
FOR PARENTS

ACKNOWLEDGEMENTS

Judith Gillham, Brenda Gardner and Ruth Williams gave relentless feedback on successive chapter drafts; Jane Cuthill word-processed the revisions at high speed.

Dr. Graham Sharp gave advice on treatment procedures in the chapter on accidents in the home.
HMSO gave permission to reproduce statistical tables from the Department of Transport Accidents Report for 1995.

For all this I am grateful.

B.G.

CHILD SAFETY
FOR PARENTS

Dr Bill Gillham

Piccadilly Press • London

Phototypeset from author's disk by Piccadilly Press.
Printed and bound by WBC, Bridgend
for the publishers Piccadilly Press Ltd.,
5 Castle Road, London NW1 8PR

A catalogue record for this book is available from the British
Library

ISBN: 1 85340 461 6

Dr Bill Gillham trained and worked as a school teacher and educational psychologist for ten years. He then worked as a course tutor and lecturer in educational psychology at Nottingham University. Since 1984 he has been a senior lecturer and course director in educational psychology at Strathclyde University. He has written many academic books including CHILD SEXUAL ABUSE (Cassell 1991), CHILD PHYSICAL ABUSE (Cassell 1994) and co-edited CHILD SAFETY: PROBLEM AND PREVENTION (Routledge 1996). He has also written a number of children's books.

This is his first book for Piccadilly Press.

CONTENTS

CONTENTS

Chapter One

CHILD SAFETY: GETTING IT RIGHT

'All advice is bad; but good advice is the worst of all':
Oscar Wilde

WHAT'S NEW?

From the very first, even before their baby is born, parents are bombarded with advice: from relatives, friends, the media, 'experts' – everyone seems to want to have their say.

But even 'good' advice is not enough. Parents have to work out what suits their case, and that means being given the facts (not always obvious) on which to base *their* decisions. An outsider – like the writer of this book – has to recognise and respect that. In any case, parents know most of what they have to do: it would be a bad world for children if they didn't. Telling them what they already know is irritating and a waste of time.

The trouble with child safety is that most of the dangers *do* seem obvious, as well as what you should do. So what is there to add? What's new?

The answer is that when you look closely at the problem we do not appear to be making a very good job of protecting our children. This book is based on new research that challenges much of what we are

1

doing at the moment. If things *aren't* improving (and this is true of many areas of child safety) maybe we're not doing it right?

THE HEADLINE PHENOMENON

Research enables us to get a *balanced* picture of child safety failures. The picture most of us have is out of balance because it is mainly based on:
• personal experience which is limited and not representative;
• news headlines: which deal with the dramatic and terrible and exceptional (otherwise they wouldn't be news).

Headline cases are of *rare events*: dreadful though they may be, the probability of these occurring is very small. There is usually a widespread reaction to the newsworthy event which quickly fades. Not always, of course; sometimes changes follow that are supposed to prevent the same thing happening again (not that they always work). The history of child protection is full of examples of this. The violent death of Maria Colwell at the hands of her stepfather in 1972 led to the widespread adoption of Child Abuse Registers to which professionals could refer because that case highlighted poor communication as a problem. But violent deaths like this still occur.

As these words are written there is a news report of a six-year-old boy abused by his mother and found murdered. There was a history of family problems and his mother had asked for him to be taken into care. The trouble is that there are tens of thousands of families like that; few cases have such a tragic outcome and it is impossible to say which they will be. It is very difficult to protect children from their own parents. Improved procedures help and there was a fall in severe injury and death rates following the general adoption of Abuse Registers. But although concern mounts when these things happen, gradually it subsides and other events take our attention.

SAFETY AND FASHION

Can there be fashions in child safety? It seems almost in bad taste to suggest such a thing. But I have heard child sexual abuse flippantly referred to as 'flavour of the month'; on another occasion a comment that bullying as a topic was 'played out' and there was 'nothing new to say'.

These anecdotes may sound cynical but they reflect reality. Different aspects and areas of child safety come into prominence and then subside: vigilance and priority vary according to these 'fashions of concern'. And yet the price of child safety is constant vigilance, a steady state of awareness and care; and a long-term *preventive* approach to improvement. When something is high profile there is a tendency to react, often in a 'quick fix' fashion, to whatever it is that has gone badly wrong. The banning of legally-held high-calibre handguns following the Dunblane tragedy is an example of this. Whether this is right or wrong morally is one issue. The practical question is: *will it prevent a future tragedy?*

BEING WISE AFTER THE EVENT

It's easy to be wise after the event: when something goes terribly wrong it always seems obvious what should have been done to prevent it. This hindsight is only of use if it leads to changes that reduce the chances of it happening again. Effective or not, changes usually don't take place for the following reasons:

• it is not clear to people what they could or should have done differently;

• the situation that went wrong may have seemed no different from hundreds of others that *didn't* end in disaster;

• although people may be specially vigilant for a while, when nothing else goes wrong they relax: until the next time;

• people resist change, even for good reasons.

PROBABILITY AND RISK

Most of us are lucky: we take risks and nothing happens. Who wants to be cautious all the time anyway? This person is always skating on thin ice, teetering on the brink, cutting it fine, etc. and nothing ever happens to him. Someone else, always cautious and careful, has had tragic things happen.

But the individual case (whether 'lucky' or 'unlucky') is misleading. If you take risks, with yourself or your children, you shorten the odds; and if you do it often enough something probably *will* happen. If you develop safety habits you lengthen the odds. The worst may still happen *but you will have done your best*. This is important. Any life has its share of failures: it is a test of our maturity how we overcome them. But the failures that are our own fault, where we didn't do our best, are the ones that stick with us. If it's only ourselves that have to bear the consequences, we can cope with that. But when somebody else, somebody dependent on us like our children, has to suffer the consequences, the pain of the guilt can be terrible. In doing your best to protect your children you are protecting yourself.

SAFETY AS A HABIT

Too often our safety precautions are temporary and reactive – either to something that's happened to us or a dramatic 'headline' event. Then we revert to our normal pattern: like crash dieting to lose weight and then reverting to normal eating habits so the weight goes back on. It is what you do normally that has a continuous effect.

If you always drive too close to the car in front you are more likely to run into one that stops suddenly. It won't happen today, or next week, or even this year, but it will almost certainly happen in the end. You may be 'lucky' and have a near-miss scare; and that may make you more cautious for a while. But if the effect is only temporary, then next time...

RARE RISKS AND COMMON RISKS

Not many of us are worried about aeroplanes landing on our house, or our children being attacked by wolves. But it is possible to get anxious about risks that are almost as unlikely to happen: especially if they've had a lot of publicity.

I remember driving to London with a colleague at a time when there had been a series of IRA bomb outrages. He was saying that he was worried about the risk (odds of millions to one) and as he did so he had some difficulty coming to a stop at a roundabout. He laughed and said: 'What I should be worrying about is the brakes on this car: there's something wrong with them!' (Odds of a few hundred to one, and perhaps less.)

It is impossible to protect yourself and your children against things that happen very rarely: there isn't enough of a pattern to guide you (or the experts). But many accidents do follow a discernible pattern – and these are the biggest risk to our children. For example, we can predict *very closely* how many children will die on the roads next year. More than that, we can predict how many child pedestrians will be injured or killed in a particular area of town. What we cannot do is say *which* children will be killed or injured. It is up to individual parents to be alert to the risks.

PARENT POWER

Parents are in charge of their own homes: they are responsible for what happens there.

But parents can feel powerless about what happens at school or in the street. You can't always be there to warn your child, support them, correct them. Nor should you be: within common-sense limits children *need* to learn to cope, and are the better for doing so. Indeed, if you are not careful, by being 'over-protective' you can make your child so fearful of the outside world that they become unable to cope with the everyday tasks of living. Far better to try to tackle the risks they run.

Parents usually *know* when things are going wrong in a school, or community, or where there is a particular risk to child pedestrians, but often feel they can't do anything about it. Parents are better placed than anyone to know about possible dangers: they have local knowledge, they know of particular incidents, and, above all, the welfare of their children is of major concern to them.

Parents have more power than they think. Child safety is a politically sensitive issue. If parents get together and provide evidence about potential dangers for politicians, administrators and other professionals the results can be surprisingly effective. There is nothing as influential as a reasonable case put forward in the proper way.

BUT WHAT ABOUT SAFETY EDUCATION?

Safety education of one kind or another is a major element in the school curriculum. Sometimes parts of it cause controversy (particularly if it deals with sex) but the general assumption is that it is a *good thing*. Road crossing, dealing with sexual abusers, drug abuse, bullying, sexual relations, safety at play and at home are all treated in greater or lesser depth. Some of the materials employed (videos, booklets, posters, puppet and theatre shows) are of a high professional standard. Children learn more about the risks and what they should do to protect themselves. Almost all of the presentations have what psychologists call 'face validity': they look as if they ought to work. And at one level they do.

When children are questioned before and after the safety programmes it's usually clear that they've learned something. Often, however, they knew quite a lot before anyway. Adult assumptions that children don't know about dangers are generally incorrect. But, in any case, knowing what they *should* do isn't enough. Do they actually *behave* more safely? The clear answer from research is: *no*.

For example, a very extensive and well-funded programme on the dangers of drug abuse mounted in secondary schools in Scotland was enthusiastically received by teachers, but follow-up showed that it had absolutely *no* effect on adolescent drug-taking behaviour.

KNOWING AND DOING

Schools are generally excellent places for acquiring knowledge and technical skills. But they are much less good at teaching life skills – skills of social survival at street-level.

We expect too much of schools because we expect too much of knowledge.

At the time of writing there is an upsurge of concern about the moral standards of young people. More is expected of parents (rightly) but more is also expected of schools: moral standards, it is asserted, should be taught. But this assumes that children don't know what they should do (almost certainly incorrect) and that teaching them will make them more morally responsible. In this area, as in most safety education, there may be a feeling that at least we would be *doing* something. Whether it would have any effect, of course, is another matter.

THE NEED FOR PARENTS TO TAKE RESPONSIBILITY FOR SAFETY TRAINING

Giving schools the responsibility for safety training is probably unreasonable; but school-based methods are also largely ineffective – although there are a few exceptions. There is, indeed, a danger in giving schools the responsibility: if parents think that the problem is being dealt with at school, they may assume that their children are more competent than they are.

Take road-crossing (the most important safety hazard) as an example. To improve what children actually do they need individual 'on-site' training in how to look for a safe place to cross and how to judge the speed and distance of oncoming vehicles. This is time-consuming and rarely practicable for primary schools – the age-range at greatest risk. The Green

Cross Code which children learn so thoroughly is of little practical help to them because they often interpret it wrongly. Something as apparently simple as using a pelican or zebra crossing requires judgements that are obvious to an adult, but not to a child. Ten per cent of all accidents to children occur on or near such crossings.

CHILDREN DON'T THINK LIKE US

All of us find some difficulty in translating 'formal' knowledge – from books or training courses – into real life. Adults are good at adapting and interpreting what they learn. Children are much less good at this: they may not see it as relevant at all, or they may apply what they know too rigidly. They also misunderstand in ways that are unexpected: for example, they may think a stranger is 'somebody nasty'. But, as we know, most dangerous strangers are very skilful at befriending children and don't fit the 'nasty' image at all.

THEORY AND PRACTICE

It may seem hard to accept that preventive safety training for children doesn't usually carry over into real life.

But you can see something exactly parallel in adults, particularly in health education. For example we all *know* the serious health consequences of: smoking, being overweight, not taking regular exercise: it doesn't necessarily mean that we change what we do. One could extend that awareness-but-lack-of-action to other areas of one's life.

Some people are better at learning the lesson than others. The same is true of children: girls are better than boys – one reason why boys are more at risk. The simplest rules work best but they often don't apply because the real world isn't that simple.

'Stranger danger' training appears to work provided children have a clear idea of what a stranger is: *anyone* you don't know, whether they're 'nice' or 'nasty' (the most dangerous strangers are 'nice').

Some American researchers carried out this kind of training with primary age children. Then they tested the children by sending them out of the class with a message for another teacher. A 'stranger' – another researcher – met the child and asked them to come to their car to bring something in. Most children said 'no', yet some children – despite training – went along. Later the researchers retrained (and re-tested) the children. Fewer went with the stranger this time, but some *still* did!

The children *knew* but they didn't *do*. Making children safe is not a simple matter even when the safe behaviour is apparently clear and straightforward. And quite often it's more complicated than that. If we are to protect our children we need:

• to know the facts (often not what you might expect);
• to understand them correctly (facts don't speak for themselves);
• above all *to find out effective ways of making our children safer*.

In some areas – like accidents in the home – this is

11

fairly straightforward; in others – like drug abuse, it is much more difficult. *But there is always something that parents can do to improve the situation.*

Chapter Two

ACCIDENTS AT HOME AND AWAY

WHERE DO ACCIDENTS HAPPEN?

Accidents mostly happen where children spend most of their time: at home before the age of five; increasingly outside at play, and especially at school and on the roads, as they get older. It doesn't mean that home is a dangerous place for young children – although it can be – just that it's where they will find the dangers that are part of everyday domestic living. Over the age of five, deaths and serious injuries mainly occur on the roads. This is a big problem in its own right and it is dealt with in a separate chapter.

WHICH CHILDREN HAVE ACCIDENTS?

All children have accidents, of course, but serious accidents resulting in death or injury follow a definite pattern and mainly occur as follows:
• *at all ages* boys are much more likely to be killed or injured than girls;
• children under five are more vulnerable than children aged 5-14, even though they are more protected;

• children and young people in the age-range 15-19 have more accidents than any other age-group *especially if they are male*;
• children from lower social classes are *many times* more likely to be accident victims than children from higher social classes – in particular, they are more likely to die in fires.

HOW MANY ACCIDENTS OCCUR?

Official statistics on deaths and serious injuries are pretty reliable – especially *deaths*: but these are the 'tip of the iceberg'. Many minor injuries go unrecorded and 'near misses' are not usually recorded at all. This is a pity because a *near-miss is an accident that could happen*. Part of a *safety audit* includes asking: where has there nearly been an accident? Too often it is not until accidents actually happen that parents, or society at large, do something. Too late for the victim.

The one exception to this wiser-after-the-event rule, though not particularly relevant to children, is in aviation. 'Near-miss' air collisions are carefully recorded and investigated and major changes often follow to reduce the risk in the future. About 200 children a year die in England and Wales as a result of accidents in the home. Three quarters of these domestic deaths occur in children under five. This figure excludes accidents outside the home and, in particular, child pedestrian (road) accidents which warrant separate attention. Fatalities apart, around 120,000 children are admitted to hospitals each year because of an accident and roughly two million are treated in

Accident and Emergency departments.

Concentrating on deaths points to the main risks but grossly underestimates the scale of the problem. Many minor injuries are dealt with at home or by GPs. A study in the late 1980s showed that almost 20 per cent of under fives had been seen by their GP as a result of an accident. And remember that this excludes 'near misses' or accidents that didn't result in injury.

HAVE THINGS IMPROVED?

Fatal accident rates are less than half what they were fifty or sixty years ago. But this improvement may be less encouraging than it seems. At all ages fewer people die as a result of illness or injury because of vastly improved medical treatment. In other words more severely injured children survive, often with disabilities that affect them for the rest of their lives.

Accident rates are, in fact, stubbornly persistent. Although they have improved over the long term they have been the main cause of child death over the age of twelve months, for the past fifty years. Sixty years ago whooping cough, now virtually eliminated, killed more children than accidents do today.

The main causes of our children dying in the 1990s are accidents and cancer; and cancer accounts for only half the number of deaths due to accidents. Accidental deaths are declining, but deaths from cancer remain the least susceptible to improvement.

WHAT ARE THE MAIN CAUSES OF ACCIDENTS IN THE HOME?

1. FIRE

Putting aside road accidents, there is a different pattern for accidents resulting in *injury* and those resulting in *death*: some causes are more dangerous than others. *Fire* accounts for almost 20 per cent of accidental deaths at home in children under twelve months and almost 50 per cent of deaths in those aged one to four years.

FIRE SAFETY

Deaths from fire have been falling steadily since the late 1980s, probably due to the wider use of smoke alarms (because there haven't been fewer fires). But although a majority of homes now have these they are often not working properly, or at all, because the batteries are in poor condition.

Fires occur most often in poorly maintained houses which are the least likely to have smoke alarms. Cooking and other domestic appliances are a major cause of fires – again maintenance and careless handling are usually to blame.

If there is a serious fire the absolute priority is to get everyone out of the house as quickly as possible – before, or at the same time as calling the fire brigade. The greatest risk to life is from fires that start at night (usually on the ground floor). Heavy smoke soon invades the hall and stairs and leaving bedroom doors open can worsen the situation. In the event of a fire like

---

this parents and children need to know *exactly* what they should do and how they should do it. This can be talked through and practised with the children. The basic procedure is for parents to go to the children and then decide the safest exit. It may be that this is out of the bedroom window (does it open easily?) at first-floor level. In modern houses with low ceiling heights it is possible to do this without risking major injury. The procedure is to close the bedroom door and put something along the bottom crack (to reduce the draught and restrict smoke), open the window and throw out bedding (duvets, pillows) to soften the fall. If there are two adults one of them goes first, hanging from the window sill and then dropping, the other adult lowering the children at arms' length and then dropping them. If there is only one adult they should lower the children first. Children should be told to bend their knees and roll as they hit the ground (like a parachutist).

Although fires are a major cause of death, *burns* account for only six per cent of injuries seen at Accident and Emergency Departments for under fives and just three per cent for the over fives. This probably reflects the obvious dangers of fires, cookers, etc. for which parents are well-prepared.

2. FALLS

The major cause of child injury in the home (and outside apart from road accidents) is *falls* of one kind or another.

3. BEING STRUCK BY AN OBJECT

Next in importance is what is usually described as *'being struck by an object'*: this covers many things, but a common occurrence is for children to run into things – especially sharp corners on furniture which are often set at a height to do maximum injury to the face and especially the eyes.

WHAT'S IN A NAME?

When doctors use the word 'infant' they mean children under 12 months. Infants under four weeks are called *neonatal*; over four weeks and under 12 months they are called *post*neonatal.

---

4. SUFFOCATION

The major cause of infant death in the home is *suffocation* – almost 50 per cent, but currently reducing as a consequence of the health promotion on sleeping position and 'safer' bedding. Suffocation also accounts for around 17 per cent of deaths between 1-4 years (various causes).

5. CHOKING

Related to suffocation is *choking*, usually on a piece of food. Although frightening for the child and parent it is rare for it to be fatal (around a dozen or so deaths a year in under fives, *most* of these infants). A piece of food obstructing the airway is the usual problem. *Prompt action by the parent is essential*. If the child *is* choking to death it will be all over before the emergency services can get there.

As a rule it is not a good idea to try to get the

obstruction out with your fingers. If it's lodged in the throat you won't be able to reach it and this may panic the child – which makes things worse. Usually the child's coughing and spluttering will bring it up. If not, turn the child upside down and strike them smartly (a good thump) between the shoulder blades. This will usually do the trick.

It is better to try to get the obstruction out than to encourage the child to get it down. In a panic it might actually go 'the wrong way' and into the lungs. Nuts are a special problem here and an operation may be necessary with the surgeon having to go in through the chest wall. Best avoided.

6. DROWNING

Death from *drowning* accounts for about 10 per cent of deaths even amongst infants and around 15 per cent amongst the rest of the under fives; after this age drowning is much more likely to occur outside the home area, and being able to swim is not a protective factor: amongst adults as well as older children, it is mainly swimmers who drown. In young children the danger can come from an ornamental fish pond – or even an untended bathtime. Again this is a situation where prompt action can save a life: see below.

RESUSCITATION TRAINING

You're at someone's house, everything normal and pleasant, and – suddenly, the 18 month old child of your host is found face down in the ornamental pond. What do you do?

Every year many people (including children) die because those around do not know how to

---

resuscitate them. Their breathing may have stopped, their heart may have stopped: but rapid (and not highly expert) action can save them.

Straightforward though it is it is *not* something you can learn from a book like this. Basic training can usually be obtained from the St. John's Ambulance Service (St. Andrew's in Scotland) or from the Chest, Heart and Stroke Association.

The key techniques are those of the 'kiss of life' – to get breathing going; and 'heart massage' – to get the heart beating again.

The importance of being able to do this is that emergency services can rarely get to the scene before death or irreversible damage occurs.

7. POISONING

Poisoning is responsible for a small number of deaths mainly in the under fives. Safety caps on most dangerous medicines and household cleaning agents have greatly reduced the risk but some children still manage to get past these – adult carelessness is the usual reason.

The most familiar poison is the nation's favourite – alcohol – and alcoholic drinks are often easily accessible and easily opened. Spirits are the main risk, because of the high concentration of alcohol in a small volume: young children become drunk on very little. Giving them water or juice to drink will reduce the concentration and the risk of harm; but better to think preventatively.

Poisoning is rarely fatal but parents can get a bad fright from a toddler's exploration in the bathroom, for example. Shampoos, conditioners and the enormous range of make-up lotions *can* be poisonous and *don't* usually have safety caps. The long list of chemical contents in your favourite shampoo can sound frightening if your child has swallowed some neat. Responsible manufacturers usually give instructions as to what to do in such cases and many add 'this product is registered with the NPIS' (National Poisons Information Service). This service, made up of seven regional centres, operates 24 hours a day and can give information and guidance on *all* substances registered with them (available to professionals only): further details are given in the Appendix. If your child does swallow something you're doubtful about, follow the instructions on the container, contact your GP or the nearest A and E Department and produce the container for the doctor to see (he/she will know about the NPIS).

WHAT ARE THE CONSEQUENCES OF ACCIDENTS?

The most severe outcome of an accident is death and that is comparatively rare. Except for the very old, everyone has a better chance of surviving an accident than 20 years ago. The extent to which the human body can be repaired – and its capacity for recovery – are remarkable, especially when you have seen the victim at the point-of-accident stage. But medical treatment cannot reverse all damage and severely injured children are often left with some degree of disability. Just what proportion is not very clear because this is a question for long term research which is difficult and expensive to do. However, one study from the mid 1980s suggests that about three per cent of children under fifteen who are admitted to hospital after an accident will suffer a permanent disability. Of course, it all depends what you mean by 'a disability'. Data from the long-term National Child Development Study gives a figure of *nine* per cent using the same criteria, and three per cent for those children seen in A and E Departments. In short, accidents are more than a matter of life or death.

WHY ARE BOYS MORE AT RISK?

One of the most puzzling questions for child safety research is why in almost all areas, and all ages, boys are much more at risk than girls. The one exception is sexual abuse, but even there the current picture (of more girls abused than boys) may be inaccurate.

• Even in children under one year boys are 35 per cent more likely to die as a result of accidents than girls.

• 50 per cent more boys than girls die from accidents in the age-range 1-4.

• More than twice as many boys than girls are killed in the age-range 5-14.

• And almost *four* times as many in the age-range 15-19.

Risk-taking behaviour is more characteristic of boys: stupidity might be another name for it, although that doesn't carry us very far. For example, *poisoning* – now much less common than it was – is almost exclusively a male prerogative. It is boys who swig bleach and other noxious substances. Clearly they need to be protected from themselves, but the paradox is that they are given more freedom than girls: and their impulsive, physically active behaviour leads them into trouble.

A side-light on this comes from research on child protection: boys are much more vulnerable to the consequences of neglect than girls. There is a lesson to be drawn here: people, generally, are more protective of girls than boys (presumably because they – incorrectly – see them as more at risk – see Chapter Three). Boys may in fact be more neglected generally.

WHAT CAN PARENTS DO TO PREVENT ACCIDENTS?

Concentrating on serious accident statistics can make it seem like a dangerous world for children. But serious accidents rarely happen, even if they are terrible when they do. In fact, bearing in mind the many *possible* risks in a normal home, it is clear that parents generally do a good job of keeping young children safe. Parents know their own territory and can usually anticipate/prevent most threats to their child's safety. But what can parents do to improve things? The main answer is to use their own expertise and special knowledge. If that sounds like the familiar pattern of the 'expert' dodging the difficult question, read on.

1. PASSIVE PROTECTION
Design and technology safety, where you don't have to think about it, is a major strand in safety at all ages. What can't happen, won't happen. Things like: dummy plugs in electrical sockets; hot water thermostats set at a 'comfortable' temperature (more important as a safety

device than a saving device); child-proof containers for medicines and other toxic substances, and child-proof locks on kitchen cupboards and tool cupboards.

2. HOW ELSE CAN WE REDUCE RISK?

Risk is a matter of probabilities. A young child whose house and garden front onto a busy road is more at risk of an accident if they should wander out than a young child living in a cul-de-sac; a child whose garden contains an ornamental fish pond or a swimming pool is more at risk of drowning. Basic decisions are involved here.

The problem is that one cannot supervise even very young children every minute of the day (you have to go to the lavatory, answer the phone, etc.)

Barriers, of one kind or another, are a basic form of protection, but they are not enough. Adults can forget to latch side gates (and children can learn how to open them); a safety gate fencing off the dangerous part of a kitchen may be left to one side for a few minutes for some very good reason. Human error is a major factor in all accidents. Of course, most of the time we are 'lucky': hundreds of times the worst doesn't happen – and then it does.

The main principle is to have a second line of defence: a cooker guard if the child *does* get near; a second (child proof) side gate.

3. DOING A SAFETY AUDIT

All the time as our children grow up we are alert to the risks – and on the lookout for new ones. Safety is not a static concept. A house and garden that is safe for a child of eighteen months may be dangerous for the same child at three. A child will suddenly discover they can climb the stairs – but getting down is not so easy; a supposedly child-proof catch will suddenly yield to the persistent manipulations of tiny fingers. This developmental aspect of safety is always ready to take us by surprise. Parents are alert to this kind of thing in an intuitive way but it is useful to note down and try to identify from knowledge of *your* child and *your* home what possible risks there are. There is usually one (or more) thing that requires priority action: taking a cool look at the whole picture focuses attention. No 'expert' can say what these priorities will be.

4. ANALYSING NEAR MISSES AND LUCKY ACCIDENTS

Doing a safety audit is an intellectual exercise: trying to anticipate dangers and preventing accidents by planning 'defences'. But children in particular, and the world in general, are not always predictable. Risks can be unexpected; but we can learn to anticipate them by being on the alert for near misses. The ratio of near misses to accidents is very great: some researchers at Nottingham University who systematically observed children's road-crossing behaviour calculated there were about a thousand near misses to one actual accident. But once is all it takes to change a child's life.

Helen Roberts, a leading researcher in this area, asked a sample of parents how they kept their children safe in less than perfectly safe surroundings. She also asked them how they identified risks. She found that almost a third of parents could think of a serious accident their child had had where they were 'luckily' not injured, and *half* the parents could think of a serious accident that *nearly* happened. Can you think of anything in your case? Or in the case of other children you know? These are the accidents 'waiting to happen' where, over time, the probabilities pile up and they *do* happen.

ACCIDENTS AWAY FROM HOME

Parents know their own home and their local scene. But a special risk for young children is when they are visiting other people's homes with their parents, *especially* if the house being visited is one where the adults don't have children or are past the age when they remember what young children are like. A prior phone call can deal with some things: other things can only be found out when you get there. This can be done unobtrusively without being a bore about it. A quick safety check should cover the following in particular:

• access to the road
• access to the kitchen/stairs
• garden paths and steps
• garden ponds/pools
• climbable things – ladders, etc.
• access to garage and garden stores
• large animals, particularly certain breeds of dog
• medicines, make-up, etc. in the bathroom
• tap water temperature (often scalding hot in 'adult only' establishments).

A similar caution applies to holidays where vigilance is often relaxed. Hotels, villas, and other leisure facilities may cater for children in the entertainment and mealtimes sense; what they often don't do is

26

cater for children in the safety sense. In general, the safety record of many resort hotels overseas leaves a great deal to be desired, and it rarely features at all in holiday brochures. Balconies are a special problem (children can often get through them, or stand up on a seat and go over them); pleasant though they are, it may be better to have a room without one. Access to roads, pool supervision, and the suitability of the sea for young children are other priorities.

Bearing in mind that *falling* and *running into things* is a common cause of injury in young children, hotels are especially dangerous, designed as they are essentially for adults and with the aim of impressing the clientele. Broad staircases with banisters that a small child can slip through, are obvious in this respect. Less obvious is the danger from the extensive use of glass for partitions and doors. These are often not made of safety glass and the eye-level markers that warn adults that there is something in the way are, of course, set at *adult* eye-level. In conditions of bright sunlight and with the excitement and distraction of novelty these may be invisible to small children, and injuries from glass are some of the worst, exceeded only by burns and scalds.

A particular risk of *scalding* comes from showers where, again abroad, there may be no safety thermostat and variations in water flow and pressure can transform a safe shower temperature into a fatal scalding level in seconds.

'Facilities for children' and 'children welcome' do not always mean that the particular needs and vulnerabilities of children have been thought through. In this area of safety, as in others, parents have to take an active role.

THE POWER OF PARENT ACTION

Holiday firms, manufacturers, service suppliers, local authorities, the police, politicians are all very sensitive to child safety issues. Failing to recognise or respond to reasonable complaints or concerns could cost them dear – in financial or reputation terms, to put their consciences no higher than that.

Parents can underestimate their power, particularly when they set about exerting it in formal, evidenced kinds of ways (letter to firms, for example, with copies to the Consumers' Association, the local Environmental Health or Trading Standards Officer – perhaps with copies to your MP or local councillor). It is necessary to be a bit public-spirited. *You* may be aware of an unsafe toy or appliance, or a dangerous 'family holiday' but other families won't be: your action could save a life or injury. Your near miss could be somebody else's accident.

HELPING CHILDREN TO PROTECT THEMSELVES

Children, and especially young children, cannot be expected to shoulder the burden of protecting themselves. But two things are helpful:
- improving their *judgement* of what is dangerous;
- making them more *skilful* in dealing with dangerous situations: as we shall see, this is particularly important when it comes to crossing roads.

A balance is necessary. We don't want to make them

fearful of the world. But it is worthwhile asking them: what do they see as dangerous? How could things be made safer? Misunderstandings are commonplace (and sometimes good ideas for improved safety can come out of this). *Children may be aware of some risks better than their parents.* Parents are not always witness to 'near accidents' – and children can be secretive about them, especially if they think they will get into trouble.

Some of the skills are *social*: how to deal with people and emergencies – for example, what to do if they need adult help, or have to call emergency services, or have to help a friend or brother or sister. At various levels safety is a habit: children need to grow up with that.

Chapter Three

PHYSICAL ASSAULT

'Television has brought back murder into the home – where it belongs': Alfred Hitchcock

CHILDREN AND PUNISHMENT

Children are most at risk of injury from their parents. Parents routinely assault their children: it's called punishment and is widely believed to be good for them. Even outside the family physical assault as punishment is often condoned. Recent cases of a policeman and a child-minder slapping an adolescent and a pre-school child respectively attracted much public approval (and a lenient official response).

Does a good slap do children any harm? Probably not, but the point is that that kind of violence is viewed differently in relation to children. If a policeman were to slap you you would be scandalised. And if a man slaps his wife, he won't get away with claiming that she needed punishment. Of course, adults need to control children. But don't adults also need to control other adults? And would assaulting them be an effective way of doing that?

There is a grey area of physical punishment in relation to children. Most of us know where the boundaries are:

30

but if it's permissible to start, under certain circumstances you might not be able to stop.

IN THE FAMILY

If a woman is found strangled the first and most obvious (and usually correct) suspect is her husband or partner. It's almost common-sense. But when a child is murdered there is a resistance to thinking, or even considering, that the parents might be involved. Don't all parents fear that something like this could happen to their child: the unknown, horrific danger you can't protect them from? It is a fear without much basis in reality.

Child murder attracts a good deal of publicity especially when the circumstances are particularly horrific, but it is a rare event. In the 5-14 age-range more children are killed on our roads in a week than are murdered in a year. Most child murders are of under fives, most of these are babies, and their parents are mainly responsible. And there are an even greater number of suspicious deaths of young children in 'home' settings where a murder charge is not brought.

FATAL CHILD ABUSE

Every few months a particularly dreadful case of a child's death in a family with a history of abuse hits the headlines. Social workers may be disciplined, investigations are carried out, experts (and those not so expert) pronounce in the media. And despite this reaction such cases continue. Deaths like this are just the tip of the iceberg; there are many more children more-or-less seriously injured in the family and even more children subjected to unacceptable levels of violence which does not result in injury. And those who are not on the receiving end themselves may be the witness of violence between their parents. Violence, like other habits, begins at home.

CAN THIS APPLY TO YOU?

It's unlikely that this applies to you in an extreme form. Most child physical abuse occurs in socially disadvantaged families: parents who are unlikely to be reading this book; *but no one is immune*. The close relationships that exist in families are uniquely stressful. That is where the strongest feelings – of love and anger – occur: Alfred Hitchcock knew what he was about.

Bringing up children is a stressful business, and it is usually a time when there are other pressures – money, work overload, conflicting demands – to cope with.

Ask yourself: have you ever hit your children unnecessarily or harder than you intended? Have you ever felt on the point of losing control? You are very exceptional if you haven't.

As you might expect, the people who are least well equipped to deal with such pressures are usually the ones who have to: the young, the poor, the unsupported.

A GLIMPSE AT HISTORY

The most surprising lesson from history is how recently children were treated publicly as well as privately, with considerable cruelty. For example, at the beginning of the last century children were commonly hanged for minor offences. Ivy Pinchbeck and Margaret Hewitt, the pioneer social historians of society's treatment of children and women, describe, in their book *Children in English Society* how 'on one day alone, in February 1814, at the Old Bailey Sessions five children were condemned to death: Fowler, aged twelve, and Wolfe, aged twelve, for burglary in a dwelling; Morris, aged eight, Solomon, aged nine and Burrell, aged eleven, for burglary and stealing a pair of shoes.'

The RSPCA was founded earlier than the NSPCC; and legislation to prevent cruelty to animals was introduced long before the 1889 Prevention of Cruelty to Children Act. This is little over a hundred years ago. Why was it so long before the state took action to protect children? Because it was felt that we do not have the right to interfere in the privacy of the family. To some extent domestic violence is still seen as a private matter, not like other kinds of criminal violence. If you see a young child being physically punished (assaulted) by a parent in the street you may not feel comfortable about it but the odds are that you won't feel you have the right to interfere.

HOW MUCH VIOLENCE IS THERE TOWARDS CHILDREN?

We don't know exactly how much violence there is towards children. Domestic violence in general and child abuse in particular is carried out in private. *Child abuse thrives on privacy*. Visibility is a big factor in the prevention of abuse.

Not all violence results in visible injury; and those injuries are not seen unless children are regularly inspected. School age children, and many preschool children in nursery are in a situation where professionals will soon detect suspicious bruising and other injuries.

The main victims of physical abuse are the under fives and, particularly, the under threes – the least visible and also the most vulnerable to assault. A ten-year-old will walk away from a blow that would kill a one-year-old, and very young children are the least 'visible' of all.

A few statistics underline this point. In 1994 ten children in the age range 5-9 were murdered in England and Wales (with another six deaths in the 'undetermined' category). In the same year 32 under-fives were murdered with a further 24 in the suspicious 'undetermined' category. A proportion of cot deaths include suspicious deaths. Contrary to popular opinion, most cases of Sudden Infant Death Syndrome (SIDS) occur in poor unmarried families and often in families with a history of child abuse.

HAVE THINGS GOT BETTER?

It is difficult to say if things have got better. The best evidence is from long-term research carried out by the NSPCC from the early 1970s up to 1990. This showed a reduction in serious and fatal injury in 0-4 year olds (the most vulnerable group) in the mid '70s when Child Abuse Registers were generally set up and an increase from the early '80s as the economy worsened. *Child abuse rates are very much affected by poverty and unemployment rates.*

CAN'T ANYONE BE AN ABUSER?

Anyone *can* be an abuser but it depends largely on your circumstances. The more protected and supported you are the less likely you are to lose control. Poverty alone is not the problem (most poor parents do not abuse their children); lack of *support* is crucial. The most vulnerable groups of parents are the young and the poor and the lone. In other words, those who are least able to cope with the pressures of managing their lives and their children, are in the most difficult circumstances. Middle-class people act to protect themselves, often putting off having children until they've established their careers and are in a stronger financial situation. Even then they find child-rearing difficult, and may find themselves behaving in a way which appalls them, but it's less likely.

WHY SUPPORT IS IMPORTANT

Support isn't just financial: it can be practical; above all it is emotional. This is particularly important to women, who are the most vulnerable to depression.

Maternal depression is a major factor in child abuse. Like most emotional states it can be seen as just something that's 'in you'. Some people do tend to become depressed more easily than others, but research carried out in the '70s showed clearly that the origins of depression in women are largely in their circumstances. *Emotional support* emerged as a key factor – whether from a partner, or a friend, or from having a part-time job where you could talk things over with other people. Some kinds of professionals – particularly Health Visitors and nursery staff – can also be important in this respect.

DEPRESSION IN WOMEN

Women are particularly vulnerable to depression at all levels of severity. At least twice as many women as men become depressed. Married women, and especially women with young children, are the most vulnerable.

Post-natal depression is a distinct variety, occurring in the months following the birth of a baby. The causes are not clear because they may not be related to external factors.

Severe depression is crippling: those who have experienced it remain vulnerable, but also learn how to deal with the warning signs.

Most depression is *reactive* – brought about by

---

break-up, sudden financial set-backs, etc. - but *protective* factors play a large part. Different kinds of emotional and practical support are the most protective of all.

HEALTH VISITORS

Although it is thinly stretched, the service from home-visiting nurses – which is what Health Visitors are – is something we take for granted. They pay regular visits in particular to mothers and young babies, and the infirm elderly. The effects of this service on child protection are under-rated because it is something we are accustomed to expect.

However, in the United States where this is *not* standard practice, research shows that vulnerable mothers who are given this kind of help treat their babies much better – less abuse, fewer accidents. Health Visitors do two important things to protect children:
• they support the mothers
• *they inspect the babies.*

This 'visibility' factor is important especially because babies are the most vulnerable to abuse.

NURSERIES AND PARENTAL SUPPORT

Nursery provision is promoted almost entirely in terms of benefits to children, despite the obvious need of many parents to work. But there are other good

reasons, of indirect benefit to children. Nurseries do these things for parents (mainly mothers):
• provide relief from child care
• provide access to professional services
• provide opportunities for socialising and meeting other parents.

All of these functions are extremely supportive. And again: they ensure that young children are 'visible' – inspected and checked in the normal course of events. *Parents know this* and it acts as a form of preventive control.

We can never predict which parents are going to abuse their children (though we know where it's most likely to occur). But *all* parents of preschool children need relief and support: an important incidental of this is that it would make abuse less likely – as well as making parents' lives easier (surely worthwhile in itself).

WHAT DOES ABUSE DO TO CHILDREN?

Violence begins at home. The truth of that is apparent when you look at the effects on children who are regularly assaulted or who witness violence between their parents (and violence and aggression don't have to be *physical*).
• Abused children are generally more aggressive than other children – and this can persist.
• Parents who abuse their children were usually abused as children themselves.

This looks a gloomy prospect, but it's not quite as bad as that. Many children from homes where there is a lot of conflict react against it. *And most children who are*

38

abused do not go on to abuse their own children. It's just that it's rare for adults who were not treated that way to maltreat their children.

IS CHILD ABUSE PREVENTABLE?

It is very difficult to change people (including oneself!) directly. People (again, including you) are largely determined by their circumstances. Somerset Maugham says somewhere that it is surprising how many people with hearts of gold were born with silver spoons in their mouth. It's not surprising at all: the character-forming qualities of adversity are much over-rated. Look at this list of known 'risk factors' for child abuse:

- family history of abuse
- criminal record
- marital discord
- low income
- unskilled or unemployed
- 'reconstituted' partnership
- 'difficult' child (boys are more difficult than girls and are more often abused)
- living in a socially disadvantaged area
- social isolation
- maternal depression.

How many of those can we do anything about (and how many apply to you)? If you feel the pressure, what about those who check out on most of these factors?

HOW DO YOU DEAL WITH CONFLICT IN YOUR FAMILY?

We come into conflict with others all the time. In shops, in public services, at work; and, above all, at home. Other people can be unco-operative, or rude, or hostile; and we get angry. There's nothing wrong with being angry and frustrated: it is the stuff of life. But how we deal with it will make things better or worse for us. Violence and aggression don't work, other than in the very short term. It can lead to a self-destructive cycle which becomes more and more of a trap: this happens to many young men in our society.

Coping, in a constructive way, with feelings of anger and frustration is something we have to learn. Children have to learn it; and they do so mainly from what they observe in the family. You have to 'model' ways of dealing with conflict. The effects are not instantaneous: it takes time and children have to grow up. Teenagers don't have the sober judgement of the middle-aged (it would be a boring world if they did). But, if they *can* learn – and temperament is a factor here – it will be because it has been demonstrated to them in the every day of family life.

It is a big responsibility. Parents who are under pressure (or put themselves under pressure) are less likely to be able to do it. You have to:
• demonstrate in your own behaviour non-violent ways of resolving conflict;
• have a 'family procedure' for managing conflict between individuals.

The essential points are these:

- it's not conflict that's wrong but how you deal with it;
- you have to calm down first (lower your voice, think about it, sit down);
- *both* sides should be heard without interruption;
- *both* sides have to offer solutions including how it could have been avoided;
- someone arbitrates, taking a *balanced* view;
- a compromise is reached, which can include an agreement to differ on some points;
- if necessary you can make a particular point to one of them on their own ('you're older than your brother', etc.).

It takes time, but learning a reasonable way of resolving conflict is one of the most important social skills of all.

THE RISK OF ASSAULT FROM OUTSIDE THE FAMILY

Physical assault by 'strangers' is rare. If a child is not assaulted by his or her parents, they are most likely to suffer at the hands of their friends or fellow-pupils at school, or those who are caring for them.

1. ABUSE BY CHILD MINDERS AND OTHERS

Children are cared for outside the family in a variety of settings: some good, some not so good. Many child minders, and nurseries in the private sector, do an excellent job but there is scope here for abuse and neglect, sometimes serious. You may have doubts, sometimes your child may appear upset, but very young children can't easily explain themselves.

Some injuries to children are so obvious that action is immediate. But most physical abuse results in simple bruising. And aren't children always falling over and bruising themselves? Bruises are easily explained away, more or less plausibly. Of course, bruises on the shins and forearms are commonplace but recurrent bruises elsewhere are suspicious *if there are a number of them*. Bruises fade very quickly:

- less than 48 hours: purplish;
- 48-72 hours: brown;
- more than 72 hours: yellow;
  Several *recent* bruises in these areas:
- head and neck
- chest and abdomen
- buttocks and *tops* of the legs
- upper arms

are definitely suspicious. You should report your concern to the local Social Services Department; what action you take about your own child is a matter for your judgement. A somewhat similar situation *can* arise with babysitters, and there is a possibility of sexual abuse here as well – especially in the case of adolescent male babysitters.

2. SAME-AGE VIOLENCE: ON THE STREET AND AT SCHOOL

Violence peaks in its worst form in the teenage years. It is teenage males between 13 and 18 years who commit most serious crimes – this has always been the case. Offences by females also peak at this age, though young men are around eight times more likely to engage in criminal violence. *Most of this violence is directed against other young men*, and your son may be victim or offender. They usually don't talk about it, because it's seen as sneaking or wimpish. But it is a very serious problem, where the police may have to be involved. How you handle any suspicions is for you to judge. Unemployed young men find it very difficult to escape the local youth culture. Further education or job-training may help here.

Violence at school, like violence in the family, has tended to be seen differently from other, more public kinds of assault. 'Bullying', which is just another word for violence, has come to be seen very differently over the past decade. But it remains the case, for example, that the police will rarely be involved when a child is assaulted by others on school premises; and this may be true of quite serious assaults requiring medical attention.

Schools themselves are *partly* to blame because whilst, on the one hand, they are becoming increasingly intolerant of violent pupils; on the other, they don't want to publicise incidents in the way that a criminal prosecution would do.

Bullying is dealt with in Chapter Six and there is no point in repeating the contents of that here, except to say that parents need to be alert to the possibility that their child is being assaulted at school. Not strangers, but family and friends are the usual culprits.

Chapter Four

CHILD PEDESTRIAN ACCIDENTS

This chapter is the longest in the book. It needs to be: no other risk to our children's safety approaches it in importance.

Few of us will know anyone whose child has been murdered; but many of us can think of someone whose child was killed or seriously injured on the road.

Currently around five thousand children a year are killed or seriously injured on our roads *as pedestrians*. A further fifteen hundred are the victims of road accidents *as passengers*, but this kind of accident is one where adults have control and must take responsibility. Children on foot have to manage the traffic environment more or less on their own: and that is when most accidents happen to them.

SOME FACTS AND FIGURES

Accident statistics for the whole of Great Britain are carefully analysed and published each year by the Department of Transport. The figures to be quoted here are from the report for 1995: they make sobering reading.

Age of Child	Killed	Seriously injured
0-4	29	626
5-7	23	834
8-11	33	1356
12-15	47	1499

Perhaps surprising is the figure for under-fives – surely the most protected group. But if they are the most protected they are also the most *vulnerable:* only a little *exposure* to road traffic is necessary for them to have an accident. The notions of 'exposure' and 'vulnerability' are important if we are to make sense of the figures: we'll come back to that.

How Do Accidents To Adult Pedestrians Compare?

Age-range	Killed	Seriously injured
0-9	69	2086
10-19	107	2946
(mostly in the under 16 age group)		
20-29	114	1406
30-39	79	929
40-49	74	766

These figures don't look good as far as children are concerned but to get an exact comparison we need to look at accident rates for different ages.

Age-range	Killed or Seriously Injured rate per 100,000 people
0-4	17
5-7	38
8-11	49
12-15	53
16-19	31
20-29	18
30-39	12
40-49	11

You can easily see that the accident rate for school-children is three or four times the rate for adults. In fact they are much more *vulnerable* than the figures show because children are not as *exposed* to traffic as adults.

EXPOSURE TO RISK

It wouldn't make sense to compare flying accident rates amongst businessmen who fly ten times or so a year with air crew who fly that many times in a week. Pilots are more *exposed* to risk (forty or fifty times) because they fly more often. So if accident rates amongst business passengers were higher that would indicate a serious (and very puzzling!) problem. *Adults cross roads far more often than children*. In particular they cross more *busy* roads. And even though they are more exposed they have a lower accident rate. In other words, children are *much* more vulnerable (more accidents on fewer road crossings). Some researchers at Nottingham University calculated that schoolchildren are *forty times* more vulnerable than adults.

ACCIDENTS AS A HEALTH PROBLEM

Accidents are the main cause of death in children over the age of one year; two thirds of these are road accidents. But they are more than a risk to life. A major health problem is the number of children who are brain-injured, or otherwise handicapped, as a result of road accidents. Medical treatment is now so sophisticated that many children survive who would have died only twenty or thirty years ago.

It is now quite common for schools to find that they have to cater for the special needs of such a child. The cost of road accidents is great in human terms but it is also substantial in economic terms. The Department of Transport calculates that the true cost of *each* road casualty is over £800,000. To that must be added all the suffering and anguish.

ARE THINGS GETTING ANY BETTER?

Serious accident rates for child pedestrians today are about two-thirds of what they were 10-15 years ago, even though there are more cars on our roads. Is all that safety education children are getting having effect? There is no reason to believe that this is the case because rates have fallen by that amount at *all* age levels except for the very old who have always been much more likely to die as a result of injuries even if they are not 'severe'. The probable reasons for the improvement are 'engineering' changes – pedestrianisation and road designs to reduce vehicle speeds. The first of these keeps pedestrians separate from traffic; the second greatly reduces the risk of serious injury and also gives the driver and pedestrian more time, and chance, to avoid each other.

THE SEX DIFFERENCE

Look at these figures for children pedestrians killed or seriously injured in 1995.

Age	Boys	Girls
0-4	435	220
5-7	566	291
8-11	901	488
12-15	863	636

A consistent finding is that in the under 12 age-group boys are twice as likely to have accidents as girls. This has always been true and is the case internationally. Even amongst the very young this is true. It is almost as if the male has a death wish. In Chapter One we commented that boys are more vulnerable to 'neglect', particularly when young. As many parents could confirm, you take your eyes off a boy and he's in trouble, and this isn't a sexist stereotype.

Why? Boys generally engage in more risk-taking behaviour but that describes what they do, it doesn't explain it. Nor does the pattern stop after childhood. As car drivers, twice as many men as women are killed in the 20-29 age-range. This greater risk is reflected in the most obvious way in insurance premiums.

WHEN DO ACCIDENTS HAPPEN?

Accidents happen when children are out on the roads. When they're in bed or in school they are not at risk.

Accident statistics show very clearly the particular danger to children when they are going to and from school. *Between 20 and 40 per cent of accidents to children occur on school journeys.* And those accident rates are *higher* amongst *older* children – presumably because parents think that at the age of nine plus children should be able to cope on their own, whereas younger children are more likely to be escorted.

There is one important point to be made here (and we'll return to it later): if children didn't have to cross traffic roads to get to school they couldn't be knocked down. This must seem like the staringly obvious but if you think it through you can see that it could have radical planning implications. The uncomfortable truth is that our present system of controlled crossings on main roads (supervised at some points by 'lollipop men/ladies') is inadequate, not least because, as we shall see, most accidents to children occur on 'quiet' unsupervised roads. Engineering changes to improve visibility for children and reduce vehicle speeds on these roads would make them safer irrespective of the age and skill of children – and such changes need not be expensive.

WHERE DO ACCIDENTS TAKE PLACE?

Busy roads are obviously dangerous: to both children and adults. And there are zebra or pelican crossings or, sometimes, underpasses – although these are expensive and can lead to other problems. Near schools there are adults in charge of crossings.

The hidden dangers for children are on the quiet minor roads they are expected to be able to cross on their own. *More than three-quarters of the accidents to young children occur here*: on roads that parents often think children can safely tackle on their own.

On these roads children have to rely on their own skills and these are often inadequate, as we shall see. There is probably no such thing as a 'safe street' for the child pedestrian.

WHAT ABOUT 'SAFE' CROSSINGS?

Anything which puts human beings in the way of oncoming traffic is putting them at risk. 'Safe' crossings (zebra, pelican, etc.) are no exception to this. Over 10 per cent of serious accidents occur to children on or near these crossings. *The figure for adults is twice that.* Does this mean that children use the crossings more carefully than adults? It does not – it's just that adults use them many times more often than children – the notion of 'exposure' again. In fact children are about twenty times more vulnerable than adults on official safe crossings. Why is that?

WHY DO CHILDREN HAVE ACCIDENTS?

There are two main reasons:

- they lack experience;
- they lack the *skilled judgement* necessary for safe road crossing.

Of course, adults make mistakes (and pay for them) but children are much more likely to get it wrong for two reasons:
- they see the problem too simply;
- they apply any rules they know too rigidly.

Let's go back to the case of road crossing.

Why Children Have Accidents On Road Crossings

Of course it's not *always* the child's fault:
- the driver might not see the red light or might not be able to stop;
- the child may be largely obscured by a stationary vehicle (when you're small you can't help that).

But, even then, with better judgement, the child might be aware that a driver is not slowing down or can't see them. Adult pedestrians are much more alert to these possibilities.

Because they are exhorted to 'find a safe place to cross' children often see official crossings as a magic carpet of safety. They also tend to run across, which makes it more difficult for drivers to see them in time. In general children don't see things from the driver's point of view. For example, they tend to think:
- that if they can see the car, the driver can see them;
- that cars can stop right away, i.e. they have no real notion of braking distance.

Some years ago I was trying to write a book on road safety for young children: the project had to be abandoned because we couldn't make it work. We tried it out with children. On one page layout we showed the 'using a crossing' problem and said 'car's can't stop right away'. One of our 'try-out' parents read the book to her six-year-old daughter and when they came to this page the little girl asked: 'Why not?'

That is a very difficult question to answer even if you have a good grasp of theoretical physics in general and the law of inertia in particular. We gave up the 'book' approach to concentrate on practical demonstration/training. More later!

The key question is: how can we improve children's skills and understanding in the *real world* of roads and traffic?

ROAD SAFETY EDUCATION

It is still the case that most road safety education takes place in the classroom. Children are taught about the hazards and what rules they should follow. They may see videos and engage in classroom activities – making posters and the like. This is changing, but in general the training is not *practical* enough. 'Real road' training does not normally figure in an already over-stretched school programme.

Because all children do receive 'road safety education' there is a danger that parents may assume children are more competent than they are.

1. THE GREEN CROSS CODE

The Green Cross Code, a short set of simple rules about road crossing, was introduced about 25 years ago. It replaced the old-fashioned Kerb Drill which dated back to 1942. This was very drill-like (Halt! Quick march!) and children were often seen to recite it at the roadside, like some magic formula that would keep them safe. The Green Cross Code is more flexible:

• First find a safe place to cross, then stop.
• Stand on the pavement near the kerb.
• Look all round for traffic and listen.
• When there is no traffic near, walk straight across the road.
• Keep looking and listening for traffic while you cross.

This seems fine at first glance although it is worth saying that adults who are skilled at road-crossing don't do it like this. The main difficulties for children are:

• deciding what is a safe place (or finding one at all);
• deciding how near or far away a car has to be for it to be safe to cross.

2. DO CLASSROOM METHODS WORK?

They increase children's knowledge about the dangers of traffic; but there is no evidence that this knowledge effectively transfers to the roadside. There has been a great deal of research on this point and it is not comforting. The best estimate is that such training might lead to a 10 per cent reduction in accidents. But it is doubtful if even this applies to children under ten.

WHAT ABOUT CHANGING THE ROAD SYSTEM?

The layout of roads in residential areas often makes them more dangerous than they need be. If pedestrians were more separated from traffic there would be fewer accidents. That is particularly true in the case of children.

If children didn't have to cross traffic roads to get to school (particularly their primary school) they wouldn't be knocked down. That may sound like pie in the sky but it is essentially a planning matter. In the Netherlands such 'pedestrian priority' areas (called *woonerven*) have been created in residential areas, with much reduced accident rates.

Pedestrianisation in the UK has mainly been of shopping areas with commercial cost-benefits, but it could be extended. There is a welcome trend to use low-cost measures to reduce vehicle *speeds* (an important factor in accidents even in towns). Road bumps, chicanes (projecting kerbs) and speed tables (noisy road surfaces) all act as 'sleeping policemen' to slow vehicles and give pedestrians more *time* and more *warning*. Time is important because one of the difficulties children have is making time/speed/distance judgements, i.e. is there time for me to get across before that car gets here? Lower speeds also mean that if there is a collision injuries are much less severe.

CHILDREN MAKING JUDGEMENTS

The time/distance problem is a good example of what young children find difficult (and even adults have to think about). *If a car is 100 metres away do I have time to get across the road?* To get this right you have to judge:

- how wide the road is
- how long it will take you to cross
- how far away the car is
- *how fast it is going.*

Adults make this sort of judgement automatically, taking into account all these factors. Children may take account of only one factor (like how far away the car is). Of course, they'll get to the adult level eventually: if they survive. *The need is for roadside training in making these judgements.*

Another difficulty for young children is seeing how things look from a different position than the one *they* are in. Many accidents happen to children who come out from behind a parked car. They have usually *seen* the car and (wrongly) assumed that the car driver has seen them when all that was visible was a child's head, low down. In poor light or wet weather the child may be invisible to the driver. *This sort of thing can be demonstrated to children when they are in the car with you,* i.e. the driver's eye view.

The time it takes for a car to stop is another thing you can demonstrate when you are driving with the child:

- *count* how long it takes (time)
- *see* how long it takes (distance) from when you start braking. You can walk them back to when you said 'Now' and pace out how far away a car has to be before it can stop for *you.*

It isn't that children are unable to make these judgements but that they need *practical* training: it is likely that only parents have the time and opportunity to do this.

LOOKING AND NOT SEEING

Children sometimes don't see the car that hit them: it was there and they looked but they didn't see it. The more complex the traffic situation the more difficult it is to see everything in a rapidly-changing scenario. Adult drivers sometimes don't see the car they collide with when, for example, they are carrying out a tricky manoeuvre like turning right out of a side road. That's a complicated situation: children are at risk in much simpler ones.

Children commonly choose bad places to cross which they assume are safe because there is not a car in sight:

- near the brow of a hill
- near a bend or junction
- where something obscures their view.

On the other hand they will sometimes hesitate to cross when a car is in sight but so far away that there is plenty of time to cross.

GIVING YOUR CHILD 'REAL ROAD' TRAINING

Children need roadside training in making judgements about *when* and *where* it is safe to cross. It is no use trying to teach this in the classroom. Parents can ask their children to 'find a safe place' when they are out with them. Any errors can then be corrected and explained in the *actual situation*. Abstract rules don't help young children: they need to see it for themselves.

The 'safe crossing places' game should be a normal safety habit for parents and children to engage in: and it takes no time at all.

HOW YOUNG CAN YOU START?

You can start teaching your children *long before they need to use the skills*. Safety routines, like all good habits, are best started *before* the child needs to use them. From the age of about three you can point out 'safe' and 'risky' places to cross and *why* this is so. And even at this age you can start them thinking about the 'time to get across' problem – the most difficult one of all for children.

What Parents Need To Teach

1. VISUAL TIMING

Adults are expert at this. They don't stop at the kerb and run through the Green Cross Code. As they prepare to cross they are watching the traffic, judging speed and distance then stepping off the kerb as a car passes, to tuck into the gap before the next car arrives. If traffic is coming from both directions they will often use the crown of the road as a central reservation before completing the crossing.

These skilled visual timing judgements are automatic for adults. Children find them much more difficult even when they think about them. You can see them hesitate and then dart out, trying to get across the road as fast as possible, as if this makes them safer. It doesn't.

You can help your child in two ways, by:

• teaching them to count in a measured way how long it takes to cross a particular road (*one banana, two bananas, three bananas, four, etc.*)

• teaching them to count how long it takes a car to reach them from a particular distance ('Start counting when it reaches the post-box.')

Again this is something you do in the *real* situation on the actual roads they are likely to cross.

2. THE 'COULD I HAVE GOT ACROSS?' GAME

Adults are more skilful road crossers than children: they've had more experience. Experience is a big factor.

Children are not as intellectually mature as adults but they can still learn and understand more 'advanced' skills if they are given training. All skills depend on a lot of practice. *Practising road crossing needs to become a habit.* As we said in the first chapter, safety is largely a matter of developing good habits. When you are out with your child you can ask them to judge for you whether you have time to get across. Use the 'counting game' to begin with, but gradually drop this and get them to tell you: 'Cross now!'. Putting *them* in charge is good practice for safety when they're on their own.

3. THE PARKED CAR PROBLEM

The Green Cross Code is fine for crossing streets that

• have very little traffic

• are not too wide

• provide a clear view in both directions.

In practice this is often impossible, even on quiet streets in large towns because the sides of the roads are lined with parked cars. It is this, in fact, which makes many supposedly quiet roads so dangerous for children. Telling children never to cross near parked cars is so much pious advice: often they don't have a choice.

One of the commonest kinds of accident is when the child comes out from behind a parked car – often darting to get across. The driver doesn't see the child until the last moment and (because of the parked cars) has little chance of avoiding them.

If children *have* to cross at these points (and often they do) empty warnings are futile. They need to be *shown* how to do it safely, i.e.:

- choose as big a gap as possible
- make sure the cars on either side are not reversing or moving off
- move out far enough to be able to see in both directions
- judge the distance (practise counting here)
- *walk* across (how long does it take?).

This is putting the responsibility on the child; but there are other things that could be pushed for by parents (in a formal way):

- banning parking on stretches of road which children regularly have to use to get to school;
- making traffic one way so that children only have to check one direction.

Such changes are remarkably difficult to achieve because of the raft of regulations that apply. But organised political muscle can do it: and parents can be the motivating force.

4. FINDING A SAFE ROUTE

A child's road-crossing journeys are mostly predictable,

centred on where they live. About a quarter of the accidents to children occur within a quarter of a mile of their home.

With your child you can work out the safest route for their regular journeys: to school, to the park, to the shops – or wherever.

• Let them show you how they usually do it (you may get some surprises).

• Where they choose an unsatisfactory place to cross ask them why they think it might be dangerous.

• Get *them* to suggest alternatives.

• When you've established a safe-crossing-place route, take them through it to practise the *is-it-safe-to-cross* routine.

• The lessons they learn from this will generalise to other, unfamiliar roads because the safety ideas are 'real', not 'theoretical'.

Habits develop slowly: children need to grow up with the safety habit.

COULDN'T SCHOOLS TEACH ROAD SAFETY?

Of course schools *could* teach road safety and a training programme recently developed by the Transport Research Laboratory is of this type and intended for use in schools. It is not yet widespread and schools are under such pressure (of time and money) we probably can't expect that this should be yet another social problem that schools have to take responsibility for. As we have stressed elsewhere in this book, we tend to expect too much of schools, too much of formal education in general.

Parents also can *individualise* safety training: they know their own child (and his or her vulnerabilities) better than anyone. Temperament and personality are factors in road accidents: the danger isn't just in the situation. But each child's situation is literally different. In coming to school they come from all directions, according to where they live. *They need to know the safest route.*

PARENT VOLUNTEERS

'Real road' training of children is labour intensive. Specially trained professionals can do it: but at a price.

Parents do a range of voluntary work in schools and with children, so what about road safety? James Thomson of Strathclyde University has compared training carried out by (trained) parent volunteers and 'experts' and found that in groups of five year olds, the parent volunteers did rather better than the experts. Since this was carried out in an area of Glasgow with a much higher than average child pedestrian accident rate, the potential effect could be considerable.

Parents reading this book who have trained their own children could think of offering their services to their local primary school for those children whose parents have not been able to do this themselves.

GETTING THE BALANCE RIGHT

The death of a child in a road accident doesn't rate national headlines: it's not newsworthy enough.

Nothing demonstrates more clearly the distorting effect of what *does* achieve the headlines.

Yet the price of our existing road system and the mix of vehicles and pedestrians takes a terrible toll on our children. Progress *has* been made but a two-pronged attack by:
• reducing traffic speeds and volumes and excluding traffic where possible,
• ensuring that *all* children have *practical* road-crossing training would reduce the rates still further.

Improving children's skills is important but not enough on its own. It's relatively cheap, of course, like most educational approaches. But it can also be seen as putting the blame onto children – if they were more careful, etc. If a child darts out from behind a parked car is it the child's fault? Isn't the situation as much to blame? And who is responsible for that?

Large costs are involved where road planning and engineering changes are involved and there could be 'inconvenience' to traffic. Quite simply although child safety is a sensitive issue children don't carry political weight: if they did the balance would be more in their favour.

Chapter Five

SEXUAL ABUSE AND EXPLOITATION

THE DISCOVERY OF SEXUAL ABUSE

Fifteen years ago child sexual abuse was an unrecognised problem in this country. Indeed, at that time, Social Work Departments did not have a separate category for it on their Child Abuse Registers. It was assumed to be something rare and nasty involving a few perverts and incestuous fathers. New research in the US in the late 1970s had highlighted the scale of the problem but, in truth, the evidence was there all the time. Data from the Kinsey Reports of the early 1950s had identified the scale of abuse at least in relation to women and girls. And there was one other major study a few years later which presented a very accurate picture of child sexual abuse. All this was to be rediscovered almost a generation later.

WHY DIDN'T WE RECOGNISE THE PROBLEM?

Medical and psychological researchers commonly find themselves in the possession of data that they know the public won't want to accept. Indeed, that their co-professionals, politicians and the media won't want to accept. So if a problem is not acknowledged by people at large there are usually two factors at work: (i) they don't know (a situation apparently easily corrected), (ii) they don't *want* to know and they close their eyes to the evidence. It is human nature – at an individual and collective level – to resist unpleasant truths.

LESSONS FROM THE PAST

Thirty-five years ago the distinguished American paediatrician, Dr. Henry Kempe, published a paper describing what he called the 'battered child syndrome': fractures, bruising, retinal damage and subdural haematomas (bleeding in the brain) in babies which resulted from abuse by parents. There was an immediate reaction: new legislation and procedures were brought into force. This may appear to contradict the previous paragraph. But Kempe's paper was not the beginning but the culmination of a process of discovery. Research papers providing evidence and voicing suspicions had been published for the previous *twenty-five years*, and nothing had been done.

Kempe described the strong resistance within the medical profession to these findings and gave credit to those who had persisted with their researches. In the area of sexual abuse the phenomenon repeated itself: there was incredulity that this sort of thing could be going on. Those researchers and professionals who took note of the US research and tried to implement the findings in their own research or professional practice soon found themselves in a complex situation – not least, the attitude that there was something odd about people who took an interest in such matters.

The Cleveland Crisis

During 1986 two paediatricians in the Cleveland Health Authority diagnosed large numbers of children as suffering from severe sexual abuse (buggery) largely on the basis of a simple test of reflex anal dilatation (the tendency of the anus to open when the buttocks are parted). Supported by members of the Social Service Department large numbers of children were admitted into care: the disruption, conflict and distress this caused were well-publicised at the time. A judicial enquiry was set up under the chairmanship of Mrs. Butler-Sloss, Q.C. Her report was published in 1988.

This is not the place to debate the rights and wrongs of that episode but a number of key points emerged:
• that obtaining evidence of sexual abuse is not easy, and that one kind of evidence is rarely adequate;
• that the paediatricians were not as careful with the evidence as they might have been and made their judgements too quickly;
• that they had to deal with much hostility;
• that errors of diagnosis were made;
• *that many children were correctly diagnosed;*
• that it was assumed (by taking the children into care) that *the abuse had occurred in the family.*

Where Does Sexual Abuse Occur?

Physical abuse mainly occurs in the family; as does child murder. In early investigations, sexual abuse occurring in the family was the most often identified;

and it was most often identified in girls. However, as more *prevalence* studies were carried out (asking a representative sample of adults if they had been abused as children and, if so, by whom) it became clear that unlike physical abuse, sexual abuse usually occurred *outside* the family, but often at the hands of known, and more-or-less trusted adults.

WHY PREVALENCE STUDIES ARE IMPORTANT

Cases that are *reported* (to the police, social services, etc.) are not typical – so that you get a distorted picture. For example, cases of child sexual abuse reported to social service departments are mainly:

- girls
- from poor homes
- abused in the family.

Studies ask a *cross-section* of people what happened to them in childhood. What you find then is:

- boys are often sexually abused
- it occurs at *all* levels of society
- it occurs mostly *outside* the family.

Step-fathers are more likely to be abusers than natural fathers but despite lurid accounts in popular works such as Louise Armstrong's 1978 book *Kiss Daddy Goodnight*, the taboo on incest appears to be quite strong. In any case heterosexual abuse of girls has been over-emphasised and the homosexual abuse of boys under-reported. Even now there is more emphasis on the effects of sexual abuse on girls rather than the effect on boys.

WHO GETS ABUSED AND BY WHOM?

Most sexual abuse is of a single incident and relatively minor. Multiple incidents tend to become progressively more serious: access to the child is a key factor here. All studies show more girls than boys experiencing sexual abuse but this is mainly because girls suffer more non-contact abuse, i.e. flashing, talking in a sexual way, showing explicit photographs, etc. The main UK study showed boys as *more* likely to have experienced contact abuse, i.e. genital manipulation to full intercourse. Boys and girls are equally likely to experience full intercourse, although girls are more likely to be the victims of incestuous abuse. The estimate for this is around 1 in 200 children which is some indication of the scale of the problem at the extreme.

AT WHAT AGE DOES SEXUAL ABUSE OCCUR?

One of the clearest findings is that abuse occurs mainly with prepubertal children – around the age of 12, or younger, in the case of boys; in girls around the age of 10 or younger. The sexual exploitation of post-pubertal but still under-age teenage girls has a different character: see later in the chapter. Paedophiles appear to prefer the smooth, hairless bodies of young children: and if this makes chilling reading the reality is a good deal more unpleasant.

WHO ARE THE PAEDOPHILES?

From prevalence studies in this country and the US it is clear that paedophiles are to be found *pro rata* at *all* levels of society. Physical abuse is part of social incompetence, or social breakdown. But it is perfectly possible to be a practising paedophile and, at the same time, socially and professionally competent.

The assumption that paedophiles are pathetic individuals who cannot cope is not the reality. Paedophiles are, incidentally, *mainly* men but not exclusively so. Female sexual abusers are uncommon but they do exist and are, in fact, less easily detected.

ARE SEXUAL ABUSERS THEMSELVES THE VICTIMS OF CHILDHOOD ABUSE?

A number of studies report that around 30-40% of convicted paedophiles claim to have been abused as children. Is there a causal link? Possibly for a minority: but the evidence is weak, because:

• around 15% of children have *some* sexually abusive experiences, but they don't become paedophiles;

• the men in these studies are not representative of paedophiles – they're the flagrant, incompetent ones who get caught;

• *it is a good case to plead, and paedophiles know it;*

• it doesn't make them any less dangerous to children.

THE PAEDOPHILE MENACE

The first chapter of this book criticised safety education programmes targeted on children because of the difficulty children have in translating knowledge into practice. But even if they were more skilled it is unlikely that they would be a match for paedophiles. One US research study asked convicted paedophiles how they procured their victims and also, usefully, what they thought children could do to protect themselves. Typically what they did was to pick out children whom they thought might prove susceptible, build up a friendship with them, and slowly develop its sexual character. Adults will recognise this as the process of seduction. Although violence is sometimes used, it is not characteristic of the 'successful' paedophile.

This social skill is matched by the kind of jobs and voluntary activities that paedophiles get themselves into so that they have privileged access to children. Teaching and child care, as well as voluntary work with children (youth groups, sports coaching, and so forth) probably have more than their share of paedophiles. Indeed, this is so common that readers may well be able to think of examples from personal experience. *The assumption that sexual abuse was mainly a family activity has blinded us to this danger from respectable professionals.*

PROTECTION FOR PAEDOPHILES

Because these are competent people they are good at keeping the children quiet (but children tend to be secretive anyway). And because they may be in positions of authority and appear perfectly normal, children's complaints are likely to be discounted (when they do make them). Other adults may be uneasy or suspicious but too uncertain or embarrassed to take any action. The level of inaction is one of the most remarkable features of this kind of case, so that paedophiles can be given immunity or protection because no one is prepared to tackle the problem. *And if adults can't cope with the subtleties how can children be expected to?* An example of this is the case of a primary school headteacher in Cornwall who systematically abused children in his school for *ten years*, even though there had been background concerns expressed by several people which led to nothing. Ultimately he was convicted of indecent assault and imprisoned.

Suspected paedophiles (such as Thomas Hamilton of Dunblane notoriety) are, of course, very good at defending themselves, and insisting on their rights, and subverting attempts to block them off from access to children.

THE NEED FOR A PAEDOPHILE 'RISK' REGISTER

Currently it is proposed that a register of convicted paedophiles be set up. How effective this might be remains to be seen, but it is limited in one important respect: to those who have been *convicted* in a criminal court. Such convictions are but the tip of the iceberg.

Criminal law is such that, the character of sexual

abuse being what it is, convictions are extremely difficult to secure. There are many such men, often with a long career of abuse. Convicted paedophiles often confess to a series of abusive incidents which may involve *hundreds* of children, some of which will have been known about. Sexual offenders (unlike many other kinds of criminals) have a long 'shelf life' and tend to remain persistent offenders.

At one level or another some of these probable (or certain) offenders are known to professionals: doctors, psychologists, social workers, the police. These concerns could be centrally registered *in the same way as concerns about parents have been recorded on Child Abuse/Protection Registers*. These registrations did not require criminal/legal standards of evidence and have served as a clearing house for concerns from different quarters.

Some adults have a question-mark over them in relation to children and this needs to be known.

WHAT CAN PARENTS DO?

This chapter has gone into the research evidence in some detail because it is important to get an accurate perspective on the problem: you can't protect your children if you don't see the problem the right way. But the question remains: if you are to protect your children, what should you do ?

• *Be aware of your own tendency to discount suspicions.* It is an unpleasant thing to entertain doubts about someone you know. But suspicions have a basis and one can become more vigilant, and perhaps check out with other parents.

- *Challenge your own uncertainty as to what to do if you feel there are grounds for suspicion.* A kind of social embarrassment is a factor here and this can apply in other safety areas. But if we see someone behaving suspiciously near locked cars or around the backs of houses we would have no hesitation in phoning the police. We wouldn't feel awkward about it. Suspicions of a possible paedophile can also be reported to the police – there is nothing illegal about it and you can remain anonymous. The police are well-used to dealing with suspicions and know how to proceed. Police forces now have special officers for precisely this kind of enquiry.

- *Be alert to adults who seek to befriend your children.* This is often done under the guise of something else (teaching them to swim, taking them camping, helping them with their homework, etc.). The questions to ask oneself are: why are they doing this? what are they getting out of it? It is common-sense for a young woman, when a man shows a friendly, helpful interest in her, to wonder whether there is a sexual dimension to it. She is not demonstrating that she has a 'nasty mind', simply exercising a little judgement and self-protection.

- *Query (at least to yourself) the sexual orientation of men who take an interest in your sons.* It is common-sense, for example, that male teachers shouldn't be involved directly with girls in activities that involve getting undressed, sleeping away from home, etc. Convention doesn't accept that, but a similar restriction should apply to homosexual or bisexual men in relation to boys. This is not being 'homophobic'. It also has to be remembered that many homosexual/bisexual men are married, so that their sexual orientation is concealed.

• *Be alert to men who invite your children to their house.* Again this is nothing to do with being chronically suspicious – just asking the questions: why? what for? and trust your intuitive doubts.

• *Be careful whom you employ as babysitters.* A significant proportion of sexual abuse is committed by babysitters – often adolescent males. The *situation* is one where abuse can occur very easily.

• *Be aware of the fact that although women are much less likely to abuse children than men, it occurs in about 3-5% of cases.* With that in mind, similar cautions as above apply.

• *Maintain an openness about sexual matters with your children.* The lack of this is one of the greatest barriers to protecting children. The notion that there *is* such an openness in our society is illusory. There is greater portrayal of sexual behaviour in the media, greater availability of pornography, more promiscuity and earlier sexual activity, but this has done little to change the furtive ambiguity of most people's attitudes to sex. Parents and children still commonly find it a difficult or impossible topic to talk about. Children sense this and know that there are some things that they cannot tell their parents. Yet disclosure is the child's best defence. This is discussed below.

• *Talk to your children about adults' possible sexual interest in them.* This follows on from the above. If you can talk about normal sexual feelings and relationships (and what people do) with your children then it becomes possible to talk about the more abnormal side of things. And if it's something you can talk about – a mentionable topic – then your child is more likely to be able to tell you things.

• *Make clear to them what are the private parts of their body.* (If your swimsuit covers it, it's private). Explain that no one should touch them there unless for good reason (doctor or nurse giving you a jab; mother or father helping you to dry yourself).

• *Explain the difference between 'good' secrets and 'bad' secrets.* Children have peculiar notions about secrets, i.e. that you don't tell them under any circumstances. Paedophiles will sometimes work on this: that they shouldn't tell 'their' secret. This can combine with the child's reluctance to disclose sexual matters so that detection of the abuse is prevented.

• *Ensure that they have a clear idea of what a 'stranger' is,* i.e. that it is *anyone* they don't know, even if they're nice and friendly. 'Stranger danger' is just *one* kind of risk: but it can be the most serious.

• *Emphasise that they go with no one, WHETHER THEY KNOW THEM OR NOT, unless they ask you first.* This rule, like the others, is simple and unambiguous, and within children's understanding. Even so, it cannot be assumed that they will always use it or apply it correctly.

• *Be alert to moody, difficult, unexplained behaviour.* This is difficult because this kind of thing is non-specific – it doesn't have one simple cause. But usually you have some idea of what lies behind the changes. Problems at school or with friends are common causes. *Bullying* (see that chapter) can have these kinds of effects. And so can sexual abuse; but in that case there are other factors that might point in that direction.

• *Soreness, redness or irritation in the genital or anal areas.* There are, of course, many reasons for this and your GP is better placed than you to make a diagnosis. Again, you may have other suspicions – in which case you should mention them to your doctor.

THE DISCLOSURE PROBLEM

One of the clearest findings from research is that children tend not to tell. Boys are, in fact, less likely to tell than girls, probably because of the usual homosexual character of the abuse and the fact that boys, generally, disclose less than girls. And the more serious the abuse the less likely they are to tell, probably partly because they feel they will be blamed and partly because they are embarrassed. Fear of the parental response is a major barrier; and not without reason. Prevalence studies, where adults are asked about their childhood experiences of sexual abuse commonly find that they have never told anyone before. And of those who *did* tell their parents many report that they were more disturbed and upset by their parents' reactions than they were by the sexual experience itself. Police, doctors and social workers come in for similar levels of criticism, although it has to be recognised that considerable changes have taken place in these professions in the handling of sexual abuse cases.

Parents can therefore have two adverse effects: they can make disclosure less likely; and they can make the effects of the abuse much worse by how they react to it.

There is no good evidence that the safety programmes children are given in school actually make them better able to protect themselves. But bearing in mind the difficulties young children have in translating what they learn into real life situations and the skilful nature of paedophiles, it seems unlikely.

However, one benefit of such programmes is that some children disclosed previous or ongoing sexual abuse as a result of the issues raised. In other words, what the programme did was to create an *atmosphere* of disclosure – conveying the message that this is something that can be talked about. Even the *language* of disclosure is important, i.e. what kind of *words* you use – words that are not 'rude' or babyish.

The US research study, mentioned earlier, where convicted paedophiles were questioned about their attitudes, asked the men what they thought was the best form of protection for children. *They said that the children should tell.* Parents also have a responsibility here because if their child discloses to them they should *themselves* disclose to the police, even if it is a friend or a member of the family. Often they do not, because of all the trouble it would cause. But what they are doing is giving the paedophile immunity, putting other children at risk. The damage paedophiles do is out of all proportion to their number, and someone has to take the initiative to stop them.

THE SEXUAL EXPLOITATION OF TEENAGERS

Paedophile interest in pre-pubertal children is different from the exploitation by older people of sexually mature (but under-age) teenagers. Girls are particularly vulnerable. The most recent large-scale survey of sexual behaviour in the UK, carried out at the end of the 80s, found that almost one in five present-day teenage girls had their first experience of sexual inter-course before the age of sixteen, compared with fewer than one in a *hundred*, forty years earlier. That, combined with the declining age for the onset of men-struation in girls (it has decreased by around two years in this century and is now typically under the age of thirteen) points to a problem that is almost self-evident.

Since having intercourse with an under-age girl is a serious criminal offence – of which men are well aware – the above figures show that we have a large-scale problem of exploitation. Even if one allows for the fact that most of these girls (by their own report) are con-senting, and even enthusiastic, partners it is nonethe-less an outright abusive situation.

With very young girls the notions of 'choice' and 'decision' and 'consent' cannot mean the same as they do in the case of an older, more experienced woman. Young girls are, in any case, sometimes hustled or pressured into sexual activity.

Roger Ingham, of Southampton University, reports that in a sample of 95 teenagers (both sexes) who were interviewed about their partner for their first experi-ence of sexual intercourse it was found that more than a quarter of them had known their partner for less than 24 hours and that half of the girls in this group had their encounter with a man at least ten years older than themselves. Indeed all girls tended to have had partners significantly older than themselves. There is no evidence that older women play much of a role in the sexual initiation of young men. But homosexual interest in under-age boys is a larger problem (most sexual abuse of boys is of this type). However, early homosexual experiences rarely determine later sexual orientation (according to recent research); the greater risk is of HIV infection. Adverse sexual experiences appear to be particularly damaging to girls and women. But there is, of course, a more extensive range of disadvantages. A major problem is the risk of pregnancy. There is a widespread assumption that teenage pregnancy rates are higher than they have ever been and are spiralling out of control. This is not correct: rates were higher in the early 1970s and have declined since then, although there was an increase in the 1980s which has reversed again in this decade. Taking a longer view, *births* per 1,000 under 20 year old women were higher in 1964 (42 per 1,000) than they were in 1994 (29 per 1,000), but there are these differences:

• there is a trend for younger teenagers to get pregnant
• most of the earlier teenage births occurred *inside* marriage
• the great majority of teenage births today occur *outside* marriage
• in 1964 there was no legal abortion, whereas now approximately 50 per cent of under 16 conceptions are terminated and around 40 per cent in teenagers as a whole.

1. WHAT CAN WE DO ABOUT IT?

A major international research study carried out in the mid-1980s pointed to possible solutions by highlighting the enormous differences in teenage pregnancy/birth-rates between countries. In particular, rates in the Netherlands were, at that time, about *one-third* the rates in England and Wales – the difference is even greater today. The researchers pointed to the greater openness about sexual matters between parents and children and in the Netherlands as a whole. The attitude is also frankly practical: adolescent sexuality is accepted as a reality and knowledge of, and *access to* contraception services, is well-developed. There is a lack of the moral ambivalence which characterises our thinking.

We live in a society where some parents keep blue movies in the wardrobe but can't talk about contraception to their children; especially their daughters.

2. IS SEX EDUCATION THE ANSWER?

The adult debate about sex education for the young routinely polarises along the dimension: 'It'll encourage promiscuity' to 'without it they can't make informed choices'. The reality is that adolescents are going to be sexually active (and vulnerable) whatever 'education' they get: and that sexual activity is rarely a matter of informed choice.

To prevent pregnancy what is needed is detailed practical advice on contraception *together with easier access to contraceptive methods that are effective and acceptable to teenagers.* Teenagers are, in fact, very contraceptive conscious but they are often caught out because of unplanned sexual activity.

It is particularly important that they should know about emergency contraception – what's available and how to get it. The Brook Street Advisory Centres run helplines for teenagers – including one about emergency contraception – details of which are given in the Appendix.

Teenage girls do not usually feel they can speak to their parents about their anxieties. Whose fault is that?

Unless you develop an open relationship on these matters your daughter may become pregnant because she has no one to turn to.

This is not simply a moral matter, but also a severely practical one. A sexually active teenager needs protection against sexually transmitted diseases (the Brook Centre advises all teenagers to use condoms) but also advice on more reliable forms of contraception – the pill, or an IUD (not usually prescribed for young women); there are many alternatives like the hormone implant *Norplant*. The book by Anne Szarewski and John Guillebaud on contraceptive methods is up-to-date and informative (details in the Appendix).

There are worse things than having a baby as a teenager, although it does normally mean relative poverty and a limiting of life chances. The alternative is to have an abortion and, as we have seen, rates for this are worryingly high and the consequences – psychologically and physically – of abortion are not clear.

No one can make moral decisions for parents; and, within limits, parents cannot make moral decisions for their children, but there is a major problem here for individual teenagers and society as a whole.

Chapter Six

BULLYING

We have always known about bullying: bullying was an unpleasant, but minor, part of school life. But children had to learn to take the rough with the smooth and stick up for themselves: in a way it was almost character-forming... And 'telling tales' about it was seen, by children as well as adults, as a pathetic form of behaviour – perhaps even less desirable than bullying itself.

DRAWING ATTENTION TO BULLYING

A number of developments emerged in the 1980s to change that perspective. The most dramatic was a small number of highly publicised suicides of school-children (mostly boys) which were attributed to persistent bullying. Suicides are, of course, the extreme edge of the effects of bullying, and in such cases there are probably other, contributing, causes. But during the past fifteen years there has been a dramatic rise in teenage suicides *particularly amongst boys and young men*. This is linked to an increase in clinical depression amongst older schoolchildren and teenagers.

'Headline' reports, as we have said before, sometimes have only short-term effects. To trigger

change, other ingredients are needed. In the late 1980s a number of elements came together so that the anti-bullying movement gathered momentum; for example:
• the attention drawn to bullying as a child safety issue by Michele Elliott's *Kidscape* programme;
• funding for a wide range of anti-bullying initiatives provided by the Calouste Gulbenkian Foundation;
• the 1989 report of the Elton Committee on discipline in schools which highlighted bullying as an issue;
• the development of UK research, particularly at Sheffield University, into bullying;
• a groundswell of opinion that aggressive behaviour *at any level* is not to be tolerated.

In short, bullying became a fashionable issue and now every school is expected to have an 'anti-bullying' policy. But is it that simple? And what exactly do we mean by 'bullying'?

WHAT IS BULLYING?

Our cultural stereotype of bullying owes much to the popular literature of the 'school stories' era of the second half of the 19th century and the first half of the present one. The pages of *Gem* and *Magnet* had their typical bullies – usually bulgy-eyed, overweight and generally unfit because of disgusting habits of furtive smoking, and the like. Tom Brown being roasted in front of the prep-room fire by Flashman and his cronies is a dominant image from the previous century.

The notion of bullying as something 'physical' dies hard. The reality is somewhat different: bullying can exist without anyone having laid a finger on the victim.

The investigation of some of the suicide cases showed that *psychological* misery rather than physical fear and torment was often the root cause. The victims' lives had become intolerable and they could see no way out of it. Bullying can be defined in the following ways:

- all types of bullying are forms of aggression;
- it may be *physical*, or *verbal* (teasing, taunting, name-calling, e.g. racist, malicious rumour-mongering), or *non-verbal* (social exclusion, gestures that imply violence);
- it involves an abuse of *power*;
- it is persistent, although a potent form is where the bully is *intermittent* in his actions.

The result is a form of *stress* where the victim knows no peace and is always more or less apprehensive.

BULLYING AND MENTAL HEALTH

This point is emphasised because *social* anxiety and a sense of *social* failure (factors in the bully-victim relationship) are major factors in the lives of adolescents. Teenagers are uniquely vulnerable to their peers, at a time in their lives when their developing sexuality and need for independence are distancing them from their parents. Depression has, until recently, been seen as an *adult* mental health problem, something that emerges as the fierce realities and pressures of life come upon you.

Having someone to confide in is very important for the prevention or alleviation of depression. The mental health risk for young men and boys is partly because they have difficulty in talking about their feelings and accepting help: it is not 'manly', and that may be a crucial obstacle to the adolescent male in trouble. He has nowhere to go so he destroys himself.

But even when the effects are not so extreme, bullying and social failure (the failure to be a member of the group and to have friends) can still have profound long-term consequences.

WHAT IS THE SCALE OF THE PROBLEM?

The answer to this is: it depends who you ask.

In the Sheffield University research teachers in upper primary schools reported that about 10 per cent of pupils were bullied to a greater or lesser extent although a fifth of the children in these schools said that they had never told a teacher when they had been bullied. Various sources report that around 5 per cent of secondary school boys are bullied. In general there is a fair measure of agreement between children and teachers as to who the bullies are.

Michele Elliott's analysis of 4,000 interviews with children aged between 5 and 16 years in UK schools found that 3 per cent of boys and 0.8 per cent of girls reported *long-term* bullying that was adversely affecting their lives. The same study found that most children had been bullied at *some* time. But it is persistent bullying that is the real source of damage.

John and Elizabeth Newson of Nottingham University found that the mothers of 25 per cent of 700 11-year-olds reported that their children were bullied in school with 4 per cent being bullied seriously. This figure is very close to the pupil-report figure in Michele

Elliott's study and suggests that parents do know what is going on.

Boiling down the results of different research investigations is a complicated business and this is not the place for it. But it is clear that serious bullying is a common problem and we can reasonably say that it affects one child in 25 or so, for a significant length of time, at some point in their lives.

BULLIES AND VICTIMS

One consistent finding is that although the number of *bullies* remains fairly constant as children get older, the number of *victims* decreases. This is probably partly a weeding out process, i.e. bullies becoming more discriminating, and partly that, at primary school, the size/power/maturity difference between the oldest and youngest children is greater than at secondary school.

But if bullying is more common in the primary school, at the secondary level it becomes more serious and difficult to eradicate. There are a number of reasons for this:
• Primary schools are smaller and teachers tend to know better what is going on.
• Children in the primary school have their 'own' teacher and are more likely to confide.
• Secondary schools are larger, more scattered places and there are more opportunities for 'concealed' bullying.
• Because they are more intellectually mature secondary-age bullies are subtler and more hurtful in

their methods.

• For similar reasons, the increasingly self-conscious victim is affected more deeply.

• Because the adolescent victim is at a greater 'distance' from both their teachers and their parents they are less likely to confide.

Of course, change is going on all the time. The victim at primary school may find himself physically growing more powerful and confident, or better able to cope. But if victims come and go, bullies tend to remain bullies. This is in line with the general finding that anti-social behaviour is remarkably persistent in children and, indeed, from childhood to adult life. It is also clear that being anti-social is itself an indicator of future mental health problems. *Bullying is as bad for the bullies as it is for the victims.*

SEX DIFFERENCES

• Boys are more likely than girls to be bullies and victims.

• Bullying by girls declines with age.

• Boys are more involved in direct, physical bullying than girls who tend to use more verbal and indirect 'psychological' bullying.

• In general, boys bully boys, and girls bully girls and use the methods which are most effective.

• It is rare for girls to bully boys, although the reverse is quite common and can take the form of sexual harassment.

WHERE DOES BULLYING OCCUR?

Bullying depends on opportunity – in those places, and at those times, where supervision is thin on the ground or absent entirely. *The level of teacher supervision has a marked effect on levels of bullying.* Going to and from school, on school buses, in toilets and changing rooms, at lesson change-over, in the playground – these all provide opportunities for the bully.

Bullying does not seem to be linked to the size of the school but the size of the *class* in secondary schools is important, and bullying is more common in schools in socially disadvantaged areas.

BULLYING AND RACIAL HARASSMENT

Whilst children from ethnic minorities are no more likely to be bullied than other children, the *form* of bullying may be different. Verbal and other 'non-contact' forms of bullying are commonly racist when directed against these children and can account for around ten per cent of incidents in a racially mixed school.

PERSONALITY FACTORS

The popular picture of the victim as socially anxious, passive, socially isolated and (in the case of boys) physically weaker than their peers is largely correct. There is also a sub group of 'provocative' victims who seem to want to invite bullying.

However, the traditional picture of the cowardly bully who is basically unsure of himself does not stand up. They are often outgoing and confident, with a good opinion of themselves; but they enjoy power and see aggression and violence as positive activities. Male bullies, however, tend not to be particularly intelligent and to have negative attitudes towards school and teachers. Female bullies, by contrast and perhaps born out by the subtle methods they use, are often intelligent and successful academically.

School Factors

It is easy to see the problem simply in terms of those kinds of pupils who are bullies and those who are victims so that dealing with the problem is targeted on those individuals (punishing them or protecting them or something in between). But bullying is not just about individuals: it is also a lot to do with the institution (school or whatever) where it occurs.

Bullying has the potential to occur at all ages and levels of society and in all institutions. In the case of adults, however, it is usually called 'victimisation' or 'harassment'.

Recently a young man has brought a civil action for damages against his former school alleging that he had suffered in mental health terms as a consequence of years of bullying at his school which failed to protect him. Without judging the rights or wrongs of the case (which are unknown to the writer) it is worth noting that the out-of-court settlement has aroused wide-spread condemnation from teachers' unions and the like. However, similar actions for damages brought, for example, by former women police officers alleging sexual harassment at work, have been settled out of court at a substantial level amongst general expressions of regret that the women should have suffered such treatment. It is also recognised that such occurrences *reflect on the management of the services involved.*

If victimisation and harassment occur at work it is seen as the fault of the management, indeed *is taken as a sign of weak management.* For a long time it has been tacitly assumed that, other things being equal, schools are more-or-less the same and that if pupils do less well or behave less well that is because of the kind of catchment area. There is a very large slice of truth in this but, increasingly, it has become apparent that schools with the same kind of catchment nonetheless achieve very different results in terms of attainment and behaviour amongst their pupils. This side of the case is commonly resisted by schools: it is easier to blame the children.

What can a parent do about this?

SCHOOL-PARENT CO-OPERATION

In an ideal world parents with a reasonable concern about their son or daughter could discuss the bullying with members of the school staff who would give a sympathetic, practical response to the problem. But parents may be too angry or upset to be reasonable. How the school staff handle this is a measure of their professionalism. Sometimes, however, parents are given a more-or-less defensive response which almost always indicates a weak case on the part of the institution. A well-managed school, like a well-managed business, is characterised in three ways:

• parents (the clients) don't make many complaints;
• the school usually *knows* the problem and is already dealing with it;
• complaints are treated as useful information and acted on swiftly.

That doesn't absolve the parents from responsibility. A parent who wants to help his or her child will do better if they:

• give themselves a chance to calm down;
• *make sure of their facts*, and check them out, if possible;
• are aware that children commonly embroider the story to make it sound more convincing;
• *put their concern in writing* whether they are going to speak to someone in the school or not (and keep a copy).

This last point is an important one because:

• it clarifies your thoughts;
• it avoids any ambiguity about what you actually said – which may be important if things get formal;
• it is harder for a school (or anyone else) to disregard a written complaint;
• if you are not satisfied with the outcome you can copy your letter to school governors or the local education authority.

If you bluster or threaten, your legitimate concerns may be swept aside because you are seen as being aggressive. The power of a reasonable, evidenced, case that is not over-stated can be remarkable. Keep a file, including notes of conversations with members of the school staff. *Write to confirm your understanding of these meetings* – good business practice again.

Parents are more powerful than they realise but they often don't go about it in the most effective way, and it is their child that bears the consequences. What has been written here is not with the intent of encouraging a 'legalistic' approach, but parents are often unevenly matched against schools and education authorities. How far the negotiation process is worth pursuing is hard to say. But the key question has to be: *are things improving for my child?*

If not, a school transfer to a school where bullying is better-managed should be considered.

WHAT DO YOU DO IF YOU SUSPECT YOUR CHILD IS BEING BULLIED?

Parents usually know, but children can sometimes feel unable to talk about the fact that they are being bullied.

If your child is moody and unhappy and, perhaps, reluctant to go to school it is sensible to talk to the school about it. Some children, particularly at the secondary stage, become 'school phobic'. This is actually not so much anxiety about going to school as anxiety at leaving home (for example, because of a possible marriage break-up), but because they are refusing school (or dragging their feet) it can seem like a school problem. Perhaps it is, perhaps it isn't: the school can soon check that out.

Whether, and at what stage, you tell your child that you have spoken to the school is up to you. Sometimes the problem can be ironed out without that being necessary. But adolescents can resent interference and on the whole it is wiser to talk to them once you know what the problem is – or have a good idea. You have to remember that children will often give reasons for not wanting to go to school which are not the real explanation. If you suspect this is the case you should ask to see an educational psychologist.

MANAGEMENT AND PREVENTION

A well-managed school is one where teachers know what is going on and problems are dealt with swiftly when they arise. Recurrent bullying is a sign that managers don't know what is going on – whether it be a school, or a prison, or a psychiatric hospital, or an army unit or a police force. Bullying thrives on slack in the system. It is not a matter of punishment but of knowing that you can't get away with things: this in itself helps prevent bullying. Bullies emerge in some kinds of institutions as in some kinds of societies; they are a sign that something is wrong.

COUNTERING BULLYING: WHAT REALLY WORKS

There has been a clutch of ideas for dealing directly with bullies – for example 'bully courts' where a group of children hear complaints from victims and, under teacher supervision, decide on sanctions for the bullies.

However, such approaches are time-consuming and artificial and of dubious value. Training in 'social skills' – such as being assertive in non-aggressive ways, although superficially sensible, doesn't seem to work in practice.

Every 'anti-bullying' initiative probably adds something to reducing the problem, but not always in the way expected: there are usually spin-offs (as in the case of sexual abuse prevention programmes which encouraged disclosure). But there are a few broad strands that appear to be most effective:
• creating a school ethos which is anti-violence and tolerant of individual differences;
• the knowledge in the school that bullying incidents will always be reported;
• the knowledge that those incidents will be dealt with swiftly and thoroughly;
• reducing opportunities for bullying.

1. ENCOURAGING 'TELLING'
One of the successes of the anti-bullying movement has been to create a climate in which children will tell: it has become acceptable to do so. Complaints by women about sexual harassment at work have been similarly affected by a climate of opinion which takes it seriously, and encourages them to report such incidents.

The key point is that *'telling' is not just up to the victim.* Children in a school know what is going on, whether they are directly involved or not. *Parents often know too.* The knowledge that it will get back effectively disarms the bully in most cases. No single change has been more important than this.

93

2. SANCTIONS AGAINST BULLIES

These need not be anything severe, but the child who tends to bully needs to know that he (or she) is known about, that his behaviour is being monitored. His parents also need to know. The bully who cannot control himself is a reasonable candidate for exclusion.

3. CREATING A CLIMATE OF TOLERANCE AND ANTI-VIOLENCE

This is a set of values that everyone has to be involved in promoting. A lot of bullying is directed against pupils who are different – not just in the most obvious ways, but because of their habits, or tastes, or personalities. It cuts across the obvious differences of race or sex. But a clear desire to promote values of tolerance and anti-violence is a subtle, multi-stranded, long-term aim.

4. REDUCING THE OPPORTUNITIES FOR BULLYING

Formal research as well as schools' own recording of bullying incidents shows up the trouble spots for bullying: some of these are easier to eradicate than others, and solutions depend upon what fits the situation and what is possible. The simplest solutions are usually the best: for example, one headteacher staggered the lunch-break for older and younger pupils so that the two groups were in the playground at different times.

5. ADULT SUPERVISION particularly by teachers who are seen as having the most authority, is most effective. This can include, for example, random checks

on school toilets (a particular focus for unpleasant bullying).

HOW YOU CAN HELP THE SCHOOL

Parents who know what schools are trying to achieve (or what they should be doing) are a formidable force. Whether it directly affects their own child or not, the reporting of incidents and backing up the school's initiatives is making the school *and the community* a safer place for their own children. A well-managed, well-disciplined school affects children's behaviour out of school as well as in – even at the level of delinquency. Promoting social values is not a slogan: it requires detailed attention and vigilance from everyone concerned.

Chapter Seven

DRUG USE AND ABUSE

This is a topic where there are no easy answers, and no answers at all unless there is a radical shift in the way we look at the problem. We start at the beginning: what we mean by the word 'drug'.

WHAT IS A DRUG?

We all know what a drug is: it is something you take by inhaling, swallowing or injecting which affects your mind and behaviour, and can turn you into an addict. That definition applies to tobacco and alcohol, the main drugs in our society, to which hundreds of thousands of adults are seriously addicted and where there is enormous cost in health and accident terms.

But, of course, they're legal and anyway we don't usually call them drugs. If we did they might frighten us more than they do. The term drugs is reserved for some medicines prescribed by doctors and for illegal substances that have similar effects to alcohol and tobacco and are used for similar purposes, that is: to make you feel good, to feel a bit 'out of yourself', to be sociable, to relieve stress and tension. If you drink to do this that is okay; if you smoke cannabis, it is not.

SHOULD ALL DRUGS BE ILLEGAL?

Our present stance on 'legal' drugs is hypocritical: cigarette packets carry health warnings and tobacco advertising is severely controlled, but you can still legally buy tobacco products. It is a criminal offence to sell them to under 16s; but it is not an offence for under 16s to smoke or possess cigarettes.

The sale of alcohol is similarly restricted, but under-age drinking is widespread. This general problem is recognised but not taken too seriously by most adults: tobacco and alcohol abuse doesn't excite such condemnation and concern as so-called drug abuse, yet it is a vastly bigger problem. All drugs can be used or abused. Few drugs do significant harm in moderate, controlled amounts; all drugs have the potential for excess and severe damage. Alcohol and tobacco are the biggest culprits but these are known drugs to older adults and so are not as frightening. There is some basis for this. Death resulting directly from drinking alcohol is very rare before middle age, whereas *sudden* deaths from drugs in adolescence are much more likely to result from taking the illicit variety. The main problem of alcohol abuse in adolescence is its link to road accidents and, in particular, crimes of violence.

One way of dealing with the devastating effects of tobacco and alcohol would be to ban them, to make them illegal. But would that do any good?

THE EFFECTS OF ILLEGALITY

The sale and consumption of alcohol is illegal in many Moslem countries where it is regarded with the same horror as we regard heroin. The religious power behind the ban gives it added force, and punishments are severe, even for non-Moslems. The only comparable example in Western society in modern times has been the period of prohibition in the United Stages during the 1920s. It couldn't be made to work and the prohibition had a number of effects:

• it made drinking an exciting activity, especially to the young and fashionable;

• it led to the production of near-lethal alcoholic drinks because there was no control of quality;

• because there was big money to be made from it, and it was illegal, organised crime took over;

• drinking brought young people into contact with the undesirables who inhabited the world of 'speakeasies' and the like;

• it gave the whole thing an aura of false glamour.

'Prohibiting' something enables you to take the moral high ground but it also means that you have no real control: only threats, warnings and punishment. If legal prohibition worked, teenagers wouldn't take drugs and there would be no drug problem: but it doesn't and they do. Similarly if teenagers abstained from sexual activities there would be no problem of unwanted pregnancies. But that is not something we can hope to achieve. The compromise is to limit the damage. This applies to teenage drug use as well. We have to learn how to live with the problem and manage it.

How Big Is The Problem?

Despite being bombarded with information we are not a well-informed society. This is because the information that comes at us is headline dominated. The exceptional and scary are news, the routine and the reassuring are not. The sudden death of a teenager from using an illegal drug is news; the eventual death of a middle-aged businessman from alcoholism is not. Drug-related deaths in the UK are approximately as follows:

- *alcohol:*   15,000 per annum (this excludes road accidents);
- *smoking*:   100,000 per annum;
- *illegal drugs:* 1,000 per annum (and only a minority of these are teenagers).

A number of surveys have shown that 25-35 per cent of secondary school pupils have *some* experience of illicit drug use; and this figure increases to almost 50 per cent as they get older. Drugs are used regularly by about 10 per cent of this age group. Cannabis and solvents are the most common, with the hard drugs (heroin, cocaine) used by around 1 to 3 per cent. It has to be emphasised that although many teenagers *try* drugs they usually find them not to their taste and stop, or only use them very occasionally, as part of socialising. Nor is it the case that they are pressured to take drugs – they want to be part of the group and they will tend to do what the group does. Social drinking is exactly the same kind of problem.

Cannabis is the most widely used illegal drug across all ages and all classes. Solvent abuse applies mainly to school-age boys and mainly in areas of social disadvantage: it's cheap and, in practice, easily obtainable.

WHAT ABOUT 'ADDICTION'?

There is a widespread notion that illicit drugs are more addictive than licit drugs. Heavy use of hard drugs can result in an addiction problem in the same way that heavy use of alcohol can. The pathetic, inadequate heroin addict almost certainly has other reasons for his inadequacy as does the hopeless alcoholic. But they are not typical of people who use either type of drug. Most people manage to use drugs and cope with their lives perfectly well: this is not the same as arguing that drug-taking is a good thing – merely that the dangers of it are much exaggerated.

THE WAR ON DRUGS

Declaring a war on drugs, like declaring war in other contexts, feels good. It feels strong and determined. But like all wars it makes the issues, and the solutions, seem simpler than they actually are.

Over the past 15 years this has happened:
• many more people have been prosecuted for possession or dealing in drugs;
• many more drugs (and smugglers) have been seized at point of entry;
• many more young people have adopted the drug habit.

If there are more prosecutions and more seizures of drug consignments it is because the market is bigger. It has done nothing to reduce the size of the problem, which has increased many times. The 'war' is being fought on too wide a front.

Over the past five or six years, an increasingly strong message from police organisations has been that some kinds of drug should be legalised – especially cannabis. The police have to enforce the law (although they are often discriminating in practice) but the scale of drug-taking means that it is a practical impossibility. Focusing on hard drugs – a more profitable market, which is also more linked to crime – would put the problem into scale and channel resources where they are needed.

As it stands, the war on drugs cannot be won.

DOES DRUG EDUCATION WORK?

If the test of drug education is whether it reduces drug-taking, the answer is *no*. This lack of effect has been known for a long time. A review of over a hundred such programmes in the US in 1980 came to this clear conclusion. More recent research in the UK confirms this. So why do we persist?

For these reasons:
• it is hard for people to believe that knowing more about the risks (or being given frightening messages about them) doesn't help;
• at least it's doing something;
• it is cheap and uncomplicated.

The assumption is that if teenagers knew the risks in a rational way they could make an 'informed' choice – which would, of course, always be not to use drugs.

There are two problems here:
• 'information' can *introduce* children to drug use;

- adolescents enjoy risky activities *particularly* when they are prohibited.

Risk-taking is something the young actively seek out – fast driving, unplanned sexual activity, a disregard for financial and other forms of security are all characteristic of the young: the reverse of the preoccupations of their anxiously ageing parents.

There are two almost unquestioned assumptions in our present-day society:

- that more information is a good thing in itself;
- that information will be used to make decisions beneficial to the individual (or group).

Both assumptions are only correct if people make their important life 'decisions' on the basis of a rational review of available information. It assumes that people are very much more rational than is, in fact, the case. The middle-aged and middle-class are more so than most, although a good deal less than they would like to think.

A common argument is: if people only knew how terrible the consequences could be, they wouldn't do it. The assumption is that people can be frightened out of their bad habits and this doesn't work: they know different. Most drug users, like most drinkers, know that the worst doesn't usually happen so that the 'horror consequences' are seen as exaggerated, or not applying to them. Scaring them off works to *some extent* with people who've never tried it. When drug-taking was a minority activity, such approaches may have had some force; when most teenagers have personal knowledge at first- or second-hand that no longer applies.

WHAT PARENTS CAN DO

1. THE PARENT-TEENAGER RELATIONSHIP

Children, and especially teenagers, can be extraordinarily secretive. In part this is because they want to be independent and to have a private life of their own. But it is also because they know there are some things they cannot talk to their parents about: *that their parents don't want to know.*

Parents who can develop a more open relationship with their teenage children are in a better position to help them and protect them. In relation to drugs a lot of the 'help' that teenagers get from parents is of the kind which maintains that barrier. In the same way that parents who develop an open relationship on sexual matters with their teenagers are better able to help them, so openness and a recognition that drug problems can arise means that their children are more likely to turn to them for help.

2. HOW PARENTS MANAGE THEIR DRUG USE IS A POWERFUL INFLUENCE

You may not like it put in that way (in which case ask yourself why), but if you demonstrate restraint and moderation in your drinking and, if you smoke, show that you are cutting down or giving up – without moralising – you are demonstrating something to your teenager. Parents who smoke are more likely to have children who smoke; and children who smoke are more likely to develop a taste for illegal drugs.

3. STOPPING THEM STARTING AND STARTING THEM STOPPING

As drug-taking has become more common and more 'normal' the first of these has become more difficult. You may have to accept that there is at least a one in three chance that your teenager will dabble in drugs at some point. You may or may not know about that. If you know or suspect it the least helpful thing is to over-react: it won't stop them and it might fence them off from your help if they need it. Probably they won't: most teenagers will experiment and then find it is not to their taste. A minority of teenagers will use drugs more regularly: again, you may or may not know. If you do know then you have to judge whether it seems to be causing them problems or not.

The most helpful thing is to maintain a dialogue with your children about drugs. It it's something you can talk about together then they are more likely to tell you when they need help.

HOW DO YOU KNOW YOUR TEENAGER HAS A DRUG PROBLEM?

There are a number of signs but most of them are *non-specific* – they could be due to other causes or the normal ups-and-downs of adolescence. So don't jump to conclusions, but look out for the following:
- sudden changes of mood
- loss of appetite
- loss of interest in school work, usual friends, hobbies, etc.

- bouts of drowsiness or sleepiness
- disappearance of money or personal belongings (that are being sold)
- lying, furtive behaviour
- unusual smells or stains on clothes
- a change in friends or companions.

SEEKING HELP

A small number of teenagers will get into difficulties and then you may need to seek professional help. Normally, your GP would be your first point of contact.

Again, the important thing is to keep your (understandable) anxiety under control. One difficult thing you may have to accept is that 'drugs' may not be the sole cause of the problem:

- There are usually other, psychological, reasons why someone becomes 'addicted' in a way which affects their ability to cope – it isn't just alcohol that creates alcoholics.
- Dependency on illicit drugs can introduce a young person to a world of minor (and sometimes major) criminals so that other bad habits develop.

Both of these are worrying. Both require specialist professional help, probably from more than one source (e.g. social work and clinical psychology).

Your family GP will often have wide experience and access to specialised services in the NHS, but there are a number of local and national agencies that deal specifically in the difficulties teenagers and their families may be experiencing. These are no more than a telephone call away. All large towns have a Drug Advice Centre: they will also know about specific local resources. See the Appendix for a list of national helplines.

The arguments in this chapter are not to be seen as 'soft' on drugs: all drugs can cause problems (whether they are legal or not). Two things are needed:

• a focus on the most seriously addictive hard drugs;
• a focus on those individuals who develop a drug habit they can't manage.

It may be difficult as a parent to deal with a teenager with a drug problem; but it is usually only parents who can support them and 'keep them together' when professional help is being sought. It is not a problem you can or will be expected to deal with on your own: but you have to manage the help and judge what will be best for your son or daughter.

APPENDIX

USEFUL ADDRESSES AND RESOURCES

1. The Royal Society for the Prevention of Accidents (ROSPA) is based in Birmingham. Address:
   Edgbaston Park
   353 Bristol Road
   Birmingham
   B5 7ST
   Tel: 0121 248 2000   Fax: 0121 248 2001
   ROSPA deals with all aspects of safety (in the workplace, etc.). Public safety, which includes safety at home and play and at school is just one of their concerns. They produce an enormous array of publications which are listed in their Public Safety catalogue (free on request). It also provides a library and information service.

2. The Child Accident Prevention Trust is based at:
   4th Floor
   Clerk's Court
   18-20 Farringdon Lane
   London
   EC1R 3AU
   Tel: 0171 608 3828
   CAPT is the only national charity that deals solely with preventing accidents and injury to children. Probably its most valuable function is the dissemination of information to parents and professionals. They produce a number of publications and also a newsletter (Child Safety Review).

3. Kidscape owes its high profile largely to its dynamic Director, Michele Elliott. It produces a wide range of publications for parents and professionals, some of which are free on receipt of a large stamped addressed envelope plus two stamps. Ring 0171 730 3300 for a publications list. Address:

Kidscape
152 Buckingham Palace Road
London
SW1W 9TR
Fax: 0171 730 7081.

The focus is essentially on developing the personal safety of children and teenagers but other aspects of child care which are problematic are also covered.

4. The National Poisons Information Service is a resource for the medical and paramedical professions only. There are seven regional centres at Belfast, Birmingham, Cardiff, Edinburgh, Leeds, London and Newcastle. The centres are open 24 hours a day to answer emergency enquiries about acute, i.e. life-threatening, poisoning. Less urgent queries are dealt with by letter. Staffing of these centres varies but normally includes nurses, pharmacists, poison specialists, and specialist doctors (who are available for clinical discussion where necessary).

This is not a service for parents, but parents need to know about it. The range of possible poisons is so great that no non-specialist can be expected to know the best treatment for all of them.

Most poisonings are not fatal but many are more-or-less harmful or, at the very least, unpleasant.

5. Sex and contraceptive education for children and teenagers. All recent research confirms that teenagers (and younger) are not getting the help and information from their schools and parents that they need.

Two very good books for teenagers and children on sex education are:

•Elizabeth Fenwick and Richard Walker (1994) *How Sex Works: A Book of Answers for Teenagers and Their Parents*, Dorling Kindersley;

•Robie H. Harris (1995) *Let's Talk About Sex*, Walker Books.

An adult book on contraception but quite suitable for teenagers is:

•Anne Szarewski and John Guillebaud (1994) *Contraception: A User's Handbook*, Oxford University Press. This is an expert, authoritative, up-to-date and clearly written reference book. You'll be surprised how much you have to learn...

6. The Brook Advisory Centres were set up specifically to give an information and clinical service to young people under 25 on contraception and related matters. The national office is at:

165 Grays Inn Road
London
WC1X 8UD
Tel: 0171 713 9000 (general enquiries)
0171 833 8488 (professional enquiries and publications)
Fax: 0171 833 8182

There is a Brook Centre in most large urban areas. There are also national helplines giving recorded information as follows:

Emergency contraception:	0171 617 0801
Missed a period?:	0171 617 0802
Abortion:	0171 617 0803
Starting contraception:	0171 617 0804
Pregnant and unsure?:	0171 617 0805
Visiting a Brook Centre:	0171 617 0806
Sexually Transmitted Diseases:	0171 617 0807

7. National helplines for drugs are as follows:
- Adfam National   0171 638 3700
- Families Anonymous   0171 498 4680
- Drugs in Schools Helpline   0345 366 666
- Drugs Helpline for the Families
  and Friends of Drug Users   01926 887 414

INDEX

READING FOR PARENTS
by Irene Yates
'...an easily digested publication of use to anyone with a child learning to read...particularly helpful for parents of reluctant readers' – Time Out

SPELLING FOR PARENTS
by Doreen Scott-Dunne
'...offers refreshingly easy strategies for parents to use with children encountering difficulties with spelling...An optimistic book which would also be useful to adults with spelling difficulties' – Independent

WELL DONE!
by Ken Adams
'Adams is particularly good at explaining maths concepts and has lots of useful strategies to impart...good value' – Time Out

WRITING SKILLS FOR PARENTS
by Irene Yates
'Irene Yates writes in a lucid style and this book is useful as much for its accessible information about how children learn as for the suggestions for enjoyable practical projects... manages to be child-, parent- and teacher-friendly simultaneously' – Time Out

Soon to be published:

OVERCOME BULLYING FOR PARENTS
by Sheila Munro
This is essential reading for all parents who worry that their child might be bullied – or be a bully.